God's Perfect Strategy

Step By Step He's Navigated My Life And Marriage

KAREN (BALYEAT) THOMPSON

ISBN: 9798447158019

DEDICATION

To my husband of 50 years! Congratulations Duane! We've had some wild and crazy times! Everyone has a story, but like ours the best. Thanks for sharing life with me.

CONTENTS

ACKNOWLEDGMENTS

To my parents, Dan and Esther. I wish you were here to read my words. I miss you dearly! For you dad, it came too late in my life to fully realize the impact you had on me. Thank you for being my steadfast dad, who was always quick to forgive.

Mom, you worked tirelessly, and yet you took the time to do all the kind motherly things. You taught me that listening is better than always having an opinion.

Thank you Duane for allowing me to spend hours on the computer, typing my heart away. Thank you for loving me, and our family.

To my niece, Angela Everett Marino, you are amazing! Your willingness to be my editor has meant the world to me. Thank you for giving me great advise without being judgemental. I couldn't have done this without you!

Thank you Natalie Kate for asking me, "Grandma, when's your book going to be done?" You have held me accountable to complete it.

Thank you Joan Shoup for being my publishing consultant.

Father God,
You listened to my prayers for help and guidance. I've always desired for this to be *our* project, not just mine. Thank you for being my guide.

INTRODUCTION

Fifty years is a long time! On our journey, we have pushed through our fair share of trials. As we age, we learn to treat each day as a gift; even including the boring and mundane tasks like grocery shopping, appointments, meal preparation, lawn work, cleaning, paying bills, etc. When we witness those who struggle with simple daily tasks, due to disease or aging, we're reminded just how fragile life can be. Every day and breath is a reason to be thankful.

Helen Keller, says it well:

"Character cannot be developed in ease and quiet. Only through experience of trial and suffering can the soul be strengthened, vision cleared, ambition inspired, and success achieved." (Keller, n.d.)

Life seems simple at times, but I courageously accept challenging, engaging, life changing experiences. My name will never be in the news or highlighted in some tabloid magazine, but better yet, if by chance you gain one piece of encouragement I'll feel most blessed. Let's live our best life, and encourage others to do the same. What I find to be the most inspiring, is knowing that our best day may be tomorrow. We don't know what lurks between sunset and sunrise.

If we wake up with anticipation to be aware of our surroundings we may just hit the jackpot for our grandest day! I believe that awareness is the key that unlocks joy.

Stop! Look! Listen! Didn't we learn that in kindergarten? I hope you'll enjoy the story of my ordinary life that feels extraordinary to me.

As you read through this memoir, I'm sure you'll find similarities to your own life. You too have a story, and someday if we meet, I'd love to hear it. I've heard it said that sometimes the most meaningful writing doesn't happen in chronological order. We will do some backtracking from time to time, so bear with me as I share my story.

FORWARD

"The thing you need to know about my mom is that she isn't afraid to challenge herself with ambitious goals, nor is she afraid of failing at them. What an admirable and exemplary trait displayed by a parent. This is a woman who has gone skydiving, ran her first half marathon and gone snorkelling with stingrays, all after the age of 50. So, it's no surprise to anyone who knows her that she is writing her first book at the spry age of 69. While these are pretty cool ticks marks on her bucket list, her truest gift and passion is that of generosity. My mom always puts others first, many times complete strangers. She has volunteered with more organizations than I can count, never being afraid to get her hands dirty, sometimes quite literally, including helping others to declutter their homes. All this is to say that I know this book is written with the same love and passion my mom has put into every other venture. With all her years of wisdom, the advice she would want to pass on to her grandchildren is to take risks, dream big, but love bigger."

Benjamin S. Thompson
Youngest son of Karen (Balyeat) Thompson

CHAPTER 1

THE BEGINNING

I was born the third of three children on June 20, 1953. Our family lived in a 1016 square foot home on the South side of Elkhart, IN. This is where my parents raised us three kids. We had three bedrooms and one bathroom for five people. The living room and kitchen were small but adequate. Frankly, I didn't know any different as most of my friends had homes about the same size. My older sister and I shared a bedroom. My brother's room was the smallest just at the end of the hallway. When my parents first bought this house it was smaller still. They added on a master bedroom after I was born.

One bathroom for five people had its challenges. I can still hear my dad saying, "When are you going to be done in there?" Lucky for my dad, there was a gas station just two minutes down the road. Every now and then dad would jump in the car and drive to the station to take care of business. He wasn't very happy when that happened.

Our basement had a poured concrete floor and cinder blocks for walls. The ceiling was low and unfinished. The washer and dryer were in the cellar and that is where mom would do her ironing. When I was little she would let me iron the pillow cases. If they weren't perfect it was still okay. I enjoyed her standing beside me and helping me learn how to iron. I liked seeing the wrinkles come out and I still do.

Our home was heated with coal for many years. The coal delivery man would travel door to door to provide the fuel that people needed. We had a coal chute door at the side of the basement where he would shovel the coal down onto the floor. Then, Dad would shovel the coal into the furnace.

As a child, and still as an adult, I have a tendency to be cold. As a kid, when I got cold I would curl up next to a floor register to get warm. One day I arrived home after school where I would wait until mom and dad got home. As usual, I was feeling chilled so I curled up next to the register. When the heat would stop running it meant the house had reached the temperature that was set on the thermostat. Every time the register would stop flowing with warm air, I would get up and turn the temperature up on the thermostat, which would cause the furnace to kick on and more warm air would come out. I kept doing this several times until the warm air made me so tired I fell asleep. By the time my mom and dad got home from work the house was so blazing hot that I got in big trouble! Lesson learned, get a blanket.

I had the best imperfect parents a kid could ask for. They worked hard. They were responsible. They loved well, and they could be a lot of fun. My parents, Dan and Esther, had a strong work ethic. My dad was in the United States Armed Forces. He served 29 months in the China-Burma-India Theater, and was awarded the Presidential Unit Citation and two battle stars for his Asiatic theater ribbon during his overseas duty.

When he returned home from the service, he went to work for C. G. Conn, and that is where he met my mom. C. G.

Conn was a major band instrument manufacturing company in Elkhart, Indiana. Together my parents made enough money to make ends meet. My dad was a trumpet buffer and I can still recall the smell of buffing compound on his clothes. My mom's job was to ream and tap instruments. In other words, she would create holes in the instruments for trumpet keys. It was hard work and sometimes monotonous. After being introduced at work, my parents had their first date on November 25, 1945. Shockingly, dad asked mom to marry him that night! My mom received her diamond on December 25,1945, and they were married March 15, 1946. It was love at first sight.

My parents wedding day

CHAPTER 2

CHOOSING THE NARROW ROAD

Every marriage has it's challenges, and my parents were no different. Early in their marriage, my dad struggled with drinking too much. When Mom confronted him about his drinking, my dad made the decision to quit. I still admire him for that! There was a local pastor, Paul Steiner, who took an interest in my parents and through his investments in their lives, they accepted Jesus Christ as their personal savior. My parents would keep that commitment to serve God until they would meet Him face to face. I'll never lose sight of the power of engagement and the work of the Holy Spirit in someone's life. Thank you Pastor Steiner!

My parents' childhood was so much different than mine. I think that's true for all of us. The world doesn't stop progressing, so changes are inevitable. My mom had three siblings and they lived very poorly. I recall my mom telling me that on one Christmas the only gift she received was an orange. Good luck trying to give your child a piece of fruit for Christmas.

My mom's parents went through a divorce which was unheard of at that time. I'm sure it's the kind of topic, back then, that women would gossip about behind closed doors. Lots of talk and little understanding, just like we tend to do today. My grandma, was sadly excommunicated from the Mennonite Church for being divorced. Boo! Hiss! But she prevailed! Yay Grandma!

My Aunt Pauline, her oldest daughter, lived right next door to Grandma as an adult. When we visited Grandma, we could also see our seven cousins. That was fun! At Aunt Pauline's, the front door was always open. Kids would be running in and out. It was the kind of house you could walk into and no one would notice there was one more kid in the house.

Over the years, Duane and I have witnessed how life is all about the choices we make. We have seen relationships, marriages, finances, careers, and health disrupted or destroyed by poor decisions. Many times those decisions lead to devastation as the ramifications snowball. Whatever we choose though, it will impact those around us. To this day, I am so grateful to have been raised in a Christian home, where my parents laid the foundation using biblical principles. It's only by God's grace, that I'm not a statistic.

The Bible says, "Enter through the narrow gate. For wide is the gate and broad is the road that leads to destruction, and many enter through it. But small is the gate and narrow the road that leads to life, and only a few find it."
Matthew 7:13-14

CHAPTER 3

THE GRANDER ONES

My Grandma Miller, my mom's mom, has a special place in my heart. Her name was Wealthy Evelina Miller. I'm not sure if the name Wealthy had any significance to my great grandparents or not. Perhaps they found her to be a gem of a girl. I'm sure she was teased about her name as a little girl, "Hey Wealthy! Can you give me some money?"

As an adult, she had a fun and mischievous smile and loved the 1960's TV show Truth or Consequences, hosted by Bob Barker. I think she was a bigger fan of Bob Barker, a nice-looking man, than the actual show. She also took a liking to Soap Operas, like the Guiding Light. When she came to our house, she liked to watch her shows. I can see her now, sitting on a footstool, just three feet in front of the TV. I'm not sure if she sat so close because of her poor eye sight or her poor hearing. Having a TV was a BIG DEAL! My parents bought our first black and white TV in 1962, when I was nine years old. I kind of like the idea that Grandma got all wrapped up in those shows. She was just like us.

For each birthday, all her grandchildren would receive a card with a one-dollar bill. That one dollar could buy some candy. Grandma was our babysitter when I was growing up. If I was sick enough to miss school, she would bring me tea and toast in bed. She also made the best peanut butter cookies! Even now, the thought of those warm cookies makes my mouth water.

Grandma liked to laugh and have fun! We spent a week together in a cabin at our church campground. At bedtime, Grandma told me to pull the blanket over my mouth so spiders wouldn't get in. I pulled the blanket over my entire head! She always prayed before we went to sleep. She should've prayed for those spiders to leave us alone!

Sometimes I would sit next to her in church. I recall one Sunday when we were singing, the old gospel hymn, *Hallelujah, Thine The Glory, Revive Us Again.* It must have been her favorite hymn. Her voice would crack as she'd tried to hit the notes. It was hard not to giggle. She always carried a big black purse. I guess she had a lot of stuff in there. We joked about being hit with the purse as she'd swing her arms around to hug us.

In her later years, she lived in an apartment complex close to downtown Elkhart. On more than one occasion, my mom and I would be going somewhere and we would see Grandma walking briskly with her big black purse and shopping bag. She loved to walk and shop. Once I got my drivers license, I'd stop by Grandma's just to visit. I was probably hoping for some of those peanut butter cookies.

Our senses play a big part in our memories. At Grandma's house, I recall the sound of creaky wooden floors, the unique wringer washer just off the kitchen and the dark steep stairs going to the second floor. I can remember the complete layout of Grandma's home, even though it's been decades ago. I cherish those memories and would love to have a chance to sit and talk with her now.

My Grandpa Benjamin Miller was a tall and thin man with a scruffy beard. His clothes smelled like burning wood, as that is how he heated his house. I'm not sure how to begin to describe my grandpa's house, but it was a shack. I'll never know why he chose to live that way. After grandpa and grandma got a divorce neither of them ever remarried.

My grandpa drove an old Model T Ford that was so out of date. His old noisy car stood out like a sore thumb. You could see and hear him coming from along ways away. Grandpa had a habit of popping in on mom and dad around suppertime. If I were outside playing and would see him driving up the street, I'd run inside and tell mom, "Grandpa's coming!" She'd set an extra place at the dinner table. He would always bring us kids pink wintergreen candies or overripe bananas. I never have liked overripe bananas, but that was his gift to us. My grandfather dug graves for a living at a cemetery right by his house in Wakarusa, Indiana. He lived in the same house that my mom and siblings grew up in until he died in a one car accident. They believe he had a heart attack. I never remember having a single conversation with Grandpa Ben. As I recall, he was a man of few words. My parents, my mom's parents, my Uncle Carl, and our granddaughter Aleigha Grace are all buried at the cemetery where Grandpa Ben dug graves. Duane and I will also be buried there. I appreciate the history that Olive Cemetery holds for my mom's family and for us.

My father came from a large family of ten kids. They were more fortunate in that my grandfather worked for the Standard Oil Company, and always had enough work.
I was in my father's childhood home many times to visit my

grandparents. My Grandma Balyeat was as short and plump as my Grandad was tall and thin. Their home was small. Several of my dad's brothers would have to share the same bed. I think the group sleep helped them keep each other warm on cold nights. My dad and several of his siblings served in the armed forces. The Balyeat family had a lot of personality. That story would require a book all of its own. All my aunts and uncles on my dad's side have passed away, but just thinking about them brings a smile to my face.

After having ten children of her own and multiple grand children, Grandma Balyeat was worn out. She would sit in her wooden rocking chair and rock away. Grandpa Balyeat would always lean up against the wall between the living room and kitchen smoking his cigarette. It still baffles me how he could hold that cigarette with such long ashes and not drop them on the floor. Grandma and Grandpa Balyeat lived close to the Elkhart Airport. When visiting them it was common to hear small planes flying overhead. One of the sounds I love to hear today is small engine planes flying over our house. They bring back fond memories.

Grandma and Grandpa Balyeat

Grandpa Miller working at the cemetery

Wealthy Miller was a gem of a lady

CHAPTER 4

MY SIBLINGS

My sister, Diana, is the oldest and, in my opinion, the strongest of us three kids. Her inner strength and determination has paid off for her. At 19 years old she diagnosed with type one diabetes, a disease that would change her life forever. One summer night, she and her best friend Carol went to McDonald's for a burger and shake. The next day Diana wasn't feeling well and complained to our mom about being so thirsty. Back in the day, our mom would read a lot from Reader's Digest, often while sitting in the beauty salon. Mom had just finished reading an article about the symptoms of diabetes and one was excessive thirst. Following her instincts, she got Diana to a doctor where they confirmed her suspicion. After spending time in the hospital getting her sugars regulated, she learned to give herself insulin injections. She has managed her diet and health with great discipline. I'm so proud of her! My sister is a kind and humble person with a beautiful soul! She loves to talk and laugh and always has fun stories to tell about her seven grandchildren.

In 1973, Diana was introduced to the love of her life, Jim Everett. They were married on March 15, 1974. Together they have two children. My brother-in-law, Jim, is a strong-minded man. He's determined and disciplined! Jim was a high school basketball star and excellent golfer. He majored in Economics in College after earning a basketball scholarship. I love and appreciate my brother-in-law.

My sister and I are six years apart, and yet we had our children within months of each other. I was always first, wink wink! I delivered Jason in November 1974 and she delivered Tony in December 1974. I delivered Ben in August of 1977 and she delivered Angie in October 1977. What are the chances of that happening? Of course we didn't plan it because that would be weird, but God did. We doubly blessed our parents!

My brother Danny is the middle child and the most talented one. He also has a remarkable memory! He remembers things Diana and I have long forgotten, or maybe have wanted to forget. He loves history, art, music and doing things for people. Dan is an amazing artist! He can draw, paint, sew, and build whatever he puts his mind to and he loves to share his creations with others. Let's just say he would do anything for you! Together, Dan and Sue have four children and they live in beautiful Wilmington, NC.

Have you ever wondered how your parents decided on a name for you? After Diana and Danny, I wonder why they didn't call be Debbie. Just sayin'.

CHAPTER 5

RUN, KAREN, RUN!

It was a beautiful summer evening. I was in grade school. My parents had made plans to go out for a nice dinner with their good friends Bernie and Marilyn. Marilyn always looked picture perfect. I had decided to go play at a friends house a few blocks away. It was out of whistle reach. When my dad wanted to get our attention he would put two fingers in his mouth, and this amazing whistle would sound the alarm for us to come home.

I had forgotten all about mom and dad's plans to go out for the evening. Something got my attention, and I suddenly remembered! We had a field behind our house which was a short cut to my friend's house. I started leisurely walking toward home through the field. As I got closer to home I could see four people standing by our backdoor. I heard this inner voice say RUN KAREN, RUN!!! Dust was flying off my little tennis shoes as I ran as fast as I could. The closer I got to home, I could see my mom and Marilyn in lovely summer dresses. When I finally came face to face with my mom, I saw the look of frustration and disappointment. She was embarrassed! I was not the image she wanted her picture perfect friend to see.

Being a Tomboy from five to ten was me. It's who I was! My sister would sit out back under the weeping willow tree and play with her dolls. That didn't seem like much fun to me. I had way too much energy for that!

CHAPTER 6

PRAY, *PLAY*, PRAY HARDER

Growing up in a Christian home was the best thing that happened to me. It gave me a sensitive spirit. I loved my parents so much that I never wanted to disappoint them. The problem became when I didn't want to disappoint my friends either. My friends often won out. Sin has a draw to it, a temporary satisfaction, often with big consequences.

My memories of grade school are mixed. My teachers were the best, but I struggled with a lack of confidence, jealousy over friendships, and wanting to please.

I started smoking in junior high, and attending parties. I'd keep my cigarettes, on a high ledge in our garage. One day as I was getting my cigarettes, I stuffed them in my coat pocket, not realizing the box was open, and turned upside down. As I left the garage, my cigarettes fell out on the ground one by one. My mom came out just in time to see it all go down. OOPS!

By high school I was smoking, drinking and partying almost every weekend. My friends and I could have a can of beer between our legs while driving down main street, flirting with the guys that drove by. The radio was cranked up playing our favorite hits. We thought we were living the high life, literally.

I tried marijuana while on spring break in Florida during my junior year of high school. My mom knew I was on a risky path. She had made arrangements for the two of us to stay with my Aunt Joyce and cousins near Cocoa Beach, FL.

The second night after mom and I arrived at my Aunt Joyce's, my cousin said to me, "We're going to the beach". A friend of hers picked us up in an old milk truck. We were the hippy generation. There were several us that went to the beach that night, including Fred, a guy who had hitched hiked to Florida from Michigan. He was super cute!

When we arrived at the beach it was dark. We all sat in a circle and they began passing the joint around. Fred, who was sitting next to me, leaned over and said, "If you don't want to do this anymore, just get up and walk away, and I'll come with you." On the second time around I looked down the beach to see someone holding a flashlight walking toward us. I got scared and walked away, Fred came with me just as he said he would.

Fred and I enjoyed each other's company so much, that he asked to take me to my junior prom. He drove from Michigan to Indiana the day of the prom. He brought everything he needed except his good shoes. UGH! He was well over 6 foot, and his shoe size was much larger than my dad's or brothers. Nevertheless, he squeezed his feet into my dad's shoes, making it painfully hard to dance the night away. We made a lovely couple both dressed in light blue.

Through my years of school there was a pattern to my life. Pray, play and pray harder. At the close of each day I would lay my head on my pillow and ask God to forgive me for all the wrong I had done. I also made God promises I didn't keep.

To make things worse, during my high school years, my parents went through a difficult time in their own marriage. Between what they were going through and my own lifestyle it could have spelled disaster. For better or for worse we all survived, and learned some hard lessons.

CHAPTER 7

FATE OR FAITH

I loved growing up in the 50's and 60's! We are the Baby Boomers! The result of all those men returning home from war time duty. It was the beginning of Rock 'n' Roll, Beatlemania, Drive-in movies, American Bandstand, Lassie, and Bonanza. It was the years of cruising Main Street, McDonalds, Bell-bottom pants and Go-go boots. Yay for the 60's!

As a senior in high school, I put together a slide show for one of my classes, using the theme song *Walk a Mile in My Shoes* by Joe South. One of the lines is, "Walk a mile in my shoes before you criticize and accuse." The slide show consisted of pictures my dad had taken of people from all walks of life. It was one of my finer moments in high school.

One of my best friend's was Karla. She and I have been friends since 7th grade. During our senior year, Karla asked me if she could have a ride home from school. As we pulled into the driveway of Karla's home, she asked me if I wanted to come inside. In the years I had known her I'd never been to her house, so I said, "Sure". As I stepped into the living room I saw two 8x10 photos, nicely framed, sitting on top of a TV stand. The one was of her oldest brother Bill and the other of her brother Duane. It was Duane's senior picture that caught my eye.

Once she saw that I was interested in knowing more about him, she told me that he was coming home the following week from Army Basic Training. She asked if I'd like her to set me up with him for a date once he got home. I said, "Yes," hoping I didn't sound too excited.

In the spring of 1971, we had our first date. When he arrived at my house and got out of his car, the first thing I noticed was how tall and handsome he was. Just like his picture! He had light brown hair and blue eyes with the longest eyelashes I'd ever seen on a man. He wore a black shirt with dark plaid pants. He made a good impression! I was looking forward to this date!

Together we decided to head up to Shula's, a local hangout in Michigan, just across the border from Indiana. I knew my friends would be there. It was a hot spot for young people where they had a bar and live music. We danced and had a great time. I would later learn he wasn't a big fan of dancing, but that night you wouldn't have known it. He was a good sport!

The drinking age in Michigan was 18 at the time. If you weren't 18 you could borrow a fake ID from a friend. In 1971 the government hadn't added photos to drivers license, making it convenient. However, it was of utmost importance to remember who you were pretending to be. It could be consequential to have your friends call you Karen while the security guard saw Debbie on your ID. Our first date went well and we went on to see each other until he had to leave for his next assignment.

Duane explained how the Army had inadvertently sent him to two wrong places, Fort Gordon, GA and Fort Mammoth, NJ. While he was in New Jersey he got word that his grandfather had passed away. His grandfather was a bigger than life figure in their family. He had been a judge for several years and was well known in his community. It was important for Duane to attend the funeral in Huntington, WV. The Army approved a leave of absence and after the funeral, his orders were to report to Fort Belvoir, VA.

Duane's job in the Army was Combat Engineering. He went on to stay at Fort Belvoir, VA for six months before being assigned to Fort Lewis, WA for another eight months. With Duane in Washington State and I in Indiana, we wrote letters, made phone calls and shared photos. We didn't have the luxury of texting or Face Time.

The picture that stole my heart

8 CHAPTER

TRANSITIONS

When life throws a curve ball, you better duck or have Jesus on your team. My parents had worked for C.G. Conn for over 20 years when the company closed its doors. This was devastating for my parents! I was a senior in high school, my brother, Danny, was in the Air Force and my sister, Diana, was in her first marriage. The only bright spot for my parents is that all of us kids were grown and able to take care of ourselves.

It didn't take long for my dad to be offered a job in Mexico, just across the border from Nogales, AZ. His job was to train Mexicans on how to buff instruments, a job he had done for many years. Moving away from Indiana was hard. My parents were born and raised here, so they were leaving everything they ever knew. They decided that my mom would stay back in Indiana until after my graduation, which was only a few months away. Then, she would move to be with Dad. They agreed to rent their home instead of selling it, in case working in Mexico didn't work out. It proved to be a wise decision. All these changes took a toll on my mom. The stress got the best of her, and she came down with a bad case of shingles in her back. I remember hearing her cry out in pain and feeling so helpless.

My dad loved Arizona, and he fit right in with the Southwest theme. He bought a cowboy hat and boots, which served him well with his fascination for snakes and wildlife. When dad was younger and a Boy Scout Leader, he taught me not to be afraid of snakes. I have a picture of a snake wrapped around my neck when I was little. It's funny how your dad can teach you to be brave by being brave himself. Some might call it risky, but I trusted my dad. I know I get my love for the outdoors, nature and the "down and out" from him.

After graduation, I shared an apartment with a good friend from high school. It was the first time I'd been on my own and I quickly learned to enjoy the independence. I made a lot of poor choices, so that book will never be written. Needless to say, I put myself in some very bad situations and I thank God for protecting me in my foolishness. We can't assume He will!

This is my dad working on the buffing machine at C.G. Conn

CHAPTER 9

READY OR NOT COLORADO

When Duane was stationed at Fort Lewis, WA, he received orders to go to Vietnam. As a combat engineer, his job could have been extremely dangerous in Vietnam. As God would have it, the Army changed Duane's orders from Vietnam to Fort Carson, CO. I believe God was paving the way for us to be married. When Duane heard his orders had changed, he called me to say he was coming home to get me.

Our dating relationship was short and sweet. He proposed to me while he was home on leave. I said, yes, and he bought me an engagement ring. That was fast! Like mother like daughter. Remember how I said my dad proposed to my mom on their first date? My head was spinning as everything was happening so fast. Duane paid off the only debt I had at a clothing store. He was Mr. Responsible, a quality that attracted me to him. He was more serious minded and had a sense of stability about him. I needed stability!

We loaded up my red Ford Pinto with a few personal items and off we went. I was 18, he was 20 and we had no plans and no money. My car chugged and chugged over the steep mountains. The Pinto wasn't calibrated to drive in high altitude. Duane had the gas pedal to the floor and it barely moved. We were relieved to arrive in beautiful Colorado. We sold my car shortly after arriving and bought a yellow

Plymouth Duster. They later banned the Ford Pinto as it became infamous for bursting into flames if the gas tank was ruptured in a collision. God was looking out for us! You'll hear more about that shortly.

We found an unfurnished apartment close to Fort Carson Army Base. We had no furniture, no beds, nothing. When Duane went to work, I stayed back in the empty apartment. There was nothing to clean, nothing to do, and no where to go. The days were long!

As I would soon learn, this man I had chosen to be my husband was going to take good care of me. He found us a furnished apartment with everything we needed. We learned quickly that our Army friends were going to be our best friends! When you're in the military, there's a bond between you. The Army becomes your family. We made many good friends and were included in weekend get togethers. Those friendships filled the void of being so far away from home.

I owned two dresses when we arrived in Colorado, a white one and a yellow one. They were both cute and appropriate for getting married by a judge. The day of our marriage, I asked Duane, "Which dress do you want me to wear? He said, "The yellow one." I chose the white one. He didn't really care, and wondered why I had bothered to ask him. In my heart I knew a bride always wears white. Even though we weren't having a big fancy wedding, that was one thing I could do to stay with tradition. I wore the white dress.

On January 28, 1972, we were married by a judge at the courthouse in Colorado Springs. Simple as simple can get.

We had just met an Army couple, Bud and Judy Robinson, days before we were married. They didn't hesitate to stand up with us as witnesses, something we needed to make the marriage official. As we took our vows, I'm sure the elderly judge had his doubts about us. His first clue to be worried was when he asked us to raise our hands, and I put my hand over my heart like I was saying the Pledge of Allegiance. I know Duane was laughing inside, but he quietly and politely corrected me. How embarrassing! To this day, all we have as a remembrance of our special day is a marriage certificate and a couple black and white photos. After all these years, it's been enough.

It is my firm belief that marriage saved by life. It took me away from a life that was going no where. It gave me a purpose. Getting married at 18, away from everything I'd ever known, boosted my confidence, it was called survival.

It was a cold winter
day on January 28,1972
but we didn't care.

CHAPTER 10

RESILIENCE

How does a boy grow up so fast? There could be many answers to this question. For my husband and his siblings, you mature fast when you lose your mother at such a young age. Duane was just 15. His mom was in her 40's when she died. Prior to her passing, she had been plagued by cancer for many years. Duane's childhood memories include frequent train trips to Huntington West VA, his mom's hometown.

His mom, Evelyn, had been in and out of hospitals and cancer treatment centers. But, through it all, she was an ambitious entrepreneur. She owned and operated Thompson Food Mart in their home town. It's my understanding that people who couldn't afford to pay for their groceries would be given an I Owe You on good faith. Over time, she and William (Bill), Duane's dad, grew apart and their marriage ended in divorce. It was a very sad and difficult time for the family. After a while, both his parents would remarry. That brought a new set of complications. One of the saddest parts of Duane's high school years was knowing his parents could never attend his football games. Every kid wants his parents to be in the stands. His mom had passed away and his dad worked crazy hours on the railroad. Perhaps it was his dad's work schedule that kept him from attending. On senior night, Duane remembers being the only player standing out on the field without a parent by his side. He promised he would never allow his sons to feel that alone. His experiences as a young person shaped the man he would become.

After just 6 weeks of marriage we would experience our first tragedy as a couple. We had just arrived home from getting groceries at the Army Commissary, when our apartment manager met up with us. He told Duane he had an emergency phone call, and needed to call his Aunt Rosemary right away. I stayed at the apartment to put groceries away and Duane walked down to the pay phone to call his aunt. We had no phone in our apartment. Minutes later, Duane returned to tell me that his dad had been killed in a one car accident. His dad was leaving work on railroad property when he hit a large chuckhole that flipped his small Volkswagen over killing him instantly. I'll never forget that date, March 15, as it was my mom and dad's wedding anniversary.

We were overcome with sorrow! It was a difficult time for Duane as he had now lost both parents by the age of 20. His heart was broken! As a new wife, it was hard for me to find the words. I remember just hugging him in our small kitchen as he wept in disbelief. After making a couple phone calls, we made flight arrangements to come home. We flew home for the funeral where I met several family members for the first time. We needed that level of support from his relatives.

On a beautiful fall evening in 1972, just months after his dad's passing we decided to drive to an outdoor movie theater located on top of a mountain. We had been there before and it was a beautiful spot! The theatre was located on a busy four lane highway. As we approached where we needed to turn, Duane noticed a car fast approaching us from behind. To avoid being hit in the rear, he quickly turned into the path of an oncoming car. We were struck hard on the passenger side. There was a couple and their two small children in the car that hit us. The windshield shattered and the engine looked like it was sitting in my lap. I was in shock and couldn't move. Duane got out of the car. Many people stopped at the accident scene to help out. We would later learn that the woman in the other car was pregnant and the guy was a sergeant in the Army. Thankfully, everyone survived serious injuries. We had glass fragments in our hair and skin and many bruises. Duane felt terrible and totally responsible! Thankfully we were driving a Plymouth Duster and not the Pinto.

Being away from family was hard. One evening we had a serious disagreement. In frustration, I got in the car and drove off. It was late, I was scared and had no place to turn. Once I swallowed by stubborn pride, I turned around and went back to our apartment. What was I going to do, wander around in the dark all night? It was a childish act on my part, but we got through it. When you're alone and far away from home, you soon realize the only place to turn is to each other. We needed those 18 months in Colorado to grow up, but it was very hard at times.

On occasion, Duane would have guard duty and be gone over the weekend. I had met a gal at my part time job, and we became good friends. Her husband had guard duty the same weekend, so she and I made arrangements to spend the weekend together at her place. When I got back to our apartment the next day, Duane was sitting in a chair with his foot propped up and a cast on his ankle. He had jumped down from his army truck during maneuvers into a large pothole and fractured his foot. He was in a cast for 6 weeks. With no phone, there was no way he could let me know until I got back home.

Army life required a lot of discipline. Duane would polish his shoes every day, and I would starch and iron his army fatigues. Thank God, Mom let me practice on those pillow cases. At 18, I didn't know much about cooking either, so Hamburger Helper was our go-to meal. Our army friends were wonderful to us! Bill and Sandy Cooley had us over to their place for our first Thanksgiving dinner as a married couple. The army wives gave me good pointers about being a newly wed. Some of them were more like moms and sisters.

Duane had hopes of getting on our local police or fire department after the army. To prepare for that he took a course in Police Science at Colorado Springs College. As part of his training he had to witness an autopsy of a young man killed in a motorcycle accident. Sometimes its easy to forget all the training men and women have to go through to be in law enforcement.

Even though Duane was state side during his military tenure, he served during one of the most tumultuous wars in our lifetime. The Vietnam conflict became increasingly unpopular as casualties and news coverage of the flighting increased. The War started in 1955 and ended in April of 1975. Four US Presidents were involved with the Vietnam

War. There were over 50,000 casualties. It was a very hard time for America as the veterans returned to an unthankful nation. Many veterans struggled with homelessness, drug addiction and mental health issues. Some have never rebounded from this tragic war.

Duane and I give a big shout out to all the men and women who have served our country sacrificially. It's easy to sit back and enjoy our freedoms without counting the cost. Our liberties have never come without a high price. One lost life or one lost limb is too many.

Duane's dad and mom,
I wish with all my heart I
could have known them.

CHAPTER 11
A FRESH BEGINNING

Duane was honorably discharged in the summer of 1973. The guys in his unit thought it would be a funny going away stunt to hold him down and shave off his mustache. Ironically, I didn't even notice it right away, even though I'd never seen him without it. To me, he was still as handsome as ever.

We loaded up our few belongings and headed back to Indiana. It was a trip Duane was hesitant to make. He would have preferred staying in Colorado, but in hindsight we believe it was the right decision. I longed to be back with family and the familiar. As a military wife, you see friends come and go as their orders constantly change. Indiana meant family, and it felt time to go home.

We lived with my parents for six months while we searched for jobs and a place to live. Duane's hopes of getting on the police or fire department didn't work out. There were no openings at the time, so my dad helped us get jobs in the factory where he worked. The work was hard and dirty, but the pay was decent. Duane stayed in the same job for 38 years! There's just not enough I can say about my husband's work ethic. He would often put in 56 hours a week and he rarely missed a day of work. I'm so proud of him!

Once we had a steady income, we bought a three bedroom house on two acres of land. Shortly after we settled into our own home, I got pregnant with Jason. There's something to be said about having your own place. Wink, wink! In August of 1974, at six months pregnant, I quit work to stay home.

It was that summer, in the quietness of my home, God began to speak to my heart. So how did God speak? It wasn't an audible voice, but it was a big tug on my heart. Big TUG! I began to examine my life, and I didn't like what I saw. Life was no longer going to be just about me and Duane. It was going to be about raising a child and being a parent. I felt humbled that God was blessing us with a baby. It was in that moment, I knew I wanted to change. I wanted God back in my life so I could be a godly wife and mother.

In those moments, when all alone, I bowed my head and recommitted my life to Christ. It was no longer going to be Pray, Play and Pray Harder. That life didn't work out for me. When someone or something becomes more important than God, we will struggle. There was a void in my life, an uneasy feeling, an itch I couldn't scratch. I was incomplete because nothing and no-one could ever fill that void except for Jesus. As a pregnant mom it was time for me to grow up, and show up!

The Bible says, "Before I formed you in the womb I knew you…" Jeremiah 1:5. God knew exactly what our son, Jason, was going to look like and be like before we did. The fascinating part of this story to me, is that God gave Jason a heart for ministry. So, the son I was pregnant with during my conversion became a pastor. WOW!
God had a plan all along. He was born on November 15, 1974. I was in labor for a long 12 hours. He was worth it!

During the time I was in delivery, the high school basketball playoffs were going on. Duane would walk down the hall to see the score of the game and sometimes I could hear hooping and hollering coming from the guys watching the game while their wives were in labor. Go figure!

Jason grew to love Jesus and sports, and it wasn't always in that order. It was a tender time for me. God was very real as He began to transform my life. Becoming a mom was the first time I felt like I had done something right in my life.

When Jason was six months old, I took on a part-time job in the evenings. Duane and I were like two ships passing in the night. It was a sacrifice we were willing to make. We didn't want to leave our first born son with anyone all day long.

We had started attending church together where I grew up. One evening while I was at work, Pastor Starkey, stopped by our home unannounced. Oh boy! It must have been something he was prompted to do. This young pastor connected with Duane and through their conversation he explained the plan of salvation. It was on that precious evening in 1975, that my husband prayed and became a born again Christian.

Duane and I later walked away from unhealthy friendships and our priorities changed. I thank God for the courage and faithfulness of that young pastor. As I reflect on this story, it sounds much like the experience my parents had. A local pastor took an interest in their lives and it made all the difference in their marriage.

We began learning to trust in God Perfect Strategy!

"For I know the plans I have for you declares the LORD, plans to prosper you and not to harm you, plans to give you hope for a future."
Jeremiah 29:11 NIV

CHAPTER 12

OVERCOMING

After three years we built a home in a subdivision. I was eight months pregnant when we moved. Benjamin was born on August 2, 1977. He came into this world three weeks late, weighing 9.1 pounds, with red hair and blue eyes. He was a big boy! My delivery was difficult with both boys. The first time I saw Ben, he had a large lump on the side of his head from all the pressure we both endured. I laid in the hospital bed that night with tears streaming down my cheeks. Our family was now complete. We had been blessed! From the day he was born we called him Benji. Now, you know that's a cute name! It fit him well.

I couldn't go to the store without someone asking me where he got his red hair. It always made for some fun conversation. We have red hair on both sides of our family, so it shouldn't have been a surprise. As a tiny baby, Benji could make us laugh. He always had a sort of worried look on his face. We wondered if that was just his look, or if he was really concerned about his new life outside the womb. Over the years, both our sons gave us many reasons to smile and laugh.

There was a large corn field behind our house owned by a neighboring farmer. The farmer's place ended up being a lifesaver in January of 1978, when our town had its largest snow blizzard that lasted several days. The blizzard was so bad it paralyzed our community. Benji was only 5 months old, and I wasn't nursing him at the time, so we needed milk for our son. We were trapped at home by the snow. We learned from our neighbors that the dairy farmer was giving away milk to whom ever needed it and could get to him. Due to the storm, the farmer had milk he couldn't deliver and if not unloaded he would have to throw it away. Duane walked through several feet of snow to the farmer's house to get fresh milk. It's a good example of neighbor helping neighbor.

After Ben was born, Duane and I agreed that I would stay at home for a while before going back to work. But several months went by and I received an unexpected call from a friend saying she was moving out of state and would I be interested in taking her job. I decided to apply for the purchasing job and ended up getting it. The company manufactured high end audio equipment and it would give me good experience. Without a college degree, this job would become a stepping stone to something better. I took the job and stayed for five years. I was planning to stay longer, but I believe God had different plans for me. It seems He often does.

It was hard leaving Benji at such a young age. There were days when I cried all the way to work. He was a mommy's boy and didn't like it when I left him at the sitters. When he cried, I would cry. It didn't take too long for him to adjust to me going to work. He adjusted much faster than I did. We had a good babysitter just down the street, so that made a world of difference in how I felt about leaving him.

On a cold winter evening in 1981, Duane, Benji and I drove to Northside Gym, a local high school, for a sectional basketball game. Jason was spending the night at a friend's house. It was playoff season. The parking lot was full so Duane dropped Benji and I off at the curb in front of the school so we wouldn't have to walk so far in the cold. While Duane was driving around looking for a parking spot, I slipped on a patch of ice and fell down hard. When I came down, I sat on my left ankle as it was twisted underneath me fracturing it in three places. Two guys, obviously unwilling to miss a second of the game, walked right past me and never said a word. BOO! A lady and her mother came up behind us and they were the ones who helped us. YAY! A nice shoutout to women helping women! Benji was only four. The ladies took his hand and held my purse until our two friends, Ross and Bob, saw what happened and came out to rescue me. Bob and Ross were waiting inside for Duane and I so we could sit with them at the game. They lifted me up and carried me inside to a table until the first responders could get to me. An ambulance was already stationed at the school in case of injuries during the game. Lucky for me!

I was soon on my way to the hospital in the ambulance. Ben waited with our friends until Duane got back from parking the car. Benji was so brave for only being four years old. The ambulance siren was on when Duane came in the school to meet me. Little did he know, I was the one in the ambulance. Duane and Benji arrived at the hospital within minutes. The X-ray showed three fractures to my left ankle. I had surgery a couple days later to attach three pins and plates. I was laid up for 6 weeks and unable to work.

Our friends and church family brought in meals and helped out where they could. What a gift!

If that wasn't bad enough, the following winter, we went to a sledding party at a nearby park. My sister and Jim were there with my niece Angie and nephew Tony. Remember those round circle sleds? My niece Angie and I decided to take it for a whirl and that is what we did. Angie was about five years old. She was in the front so I was holding on to her. As we headed down the icy snow covered hill our sled started to head right toward a fence at the side of the hill. To stop us from hitting the fence head on, I dug my heels into the snow to slow us down, but instead the sled spun us around until my back hit a metal fence pole. As I tried to roll off the sled I discovered I was in excruciating pain. Not again!!!

I laid at the bottom of a hill until the ambulance arrived. I'm sure I was well loved for ruining everyone's snow day at the park. The X-ray showed broken bone spurs at the bottom of my vertebrae. After several days in the hospital, I went home with minimal mobility. If you've ever fractured a rib, that is what it felt like. It was during this time that my boss found a replacement for me. Sad face! Thankfully I hadn't lost my employment, and was given another position. Talk about getting kicked when your down! My boss gave me a "floaters job". There's nothing secure when you're a floater. Down deep in my heart I was hurt. How could she do this to me at such a fragile time? I started looking for a new job. My mom worked at Miles Laboratories, one of the best places to work in our area at that time. She encouraged me to apply there. I did and was hired shortly after. When I told my boss that I had a new job and would be quitting, it felt good! I worked at Miles/Bayer for 33 years until retirement.

During the 1970's, we had a lot to overcome. Scripture says in Romans 8:28, "And we know that all things work together for the good to them that love God, to them who are called according to his purpose." KSV

This verse has proven to be true over and over again in our lives.

CHAPTER 13

MY STEADFAST DAD

In May 1984, I started my new job at Miles Laboratories (Bayer Healthcare). The people were easy to like and my boss was a good family man. Life was going fairly well. We were busy with the boys' activities, our church involvement and our jobs. Then several years later, in 1988, my dad became ill. One evening my parents stopped by our house unexpectedly. They had been out shopping when mom noticed dad having trouble walking and he wasn't able to smile right. Simply put, his smile was slanted. When we saw dad, we knew something was wrong. He tried to make light of it, but it was serious.

After extensive tests and scans, doctors determined that dad had a brain tumor. Local doctors decided it would be best for him to be seen by the experts at Mayo Clinic in Rochester, MN. He was flown by helicopter to Mayo with my mom by his side. It was quite an ordeal for mom sitting in the front seat of the helicopter and not knowing the extent of dad's tumor.

Shortly after Mom and Dad arrived at Mayo Clinic, I had one of those aha moments. After work one evening, I sat on a barstool in our kitchen with my head in my hands, so heart broken that my mom was alone at the clinic. It's one of those times in my life where I had an overwhelming sense of what I needed to do. I told Duane, "I have to go to be with my mom." Jason and Ben were sitting on each side of me.

They didn't say a word, but I knew they were concerned as well. Duane gave me his full support and blessing. I scheduled a flight to Rochester.

When I arrived, I went to the clinic to meet mom. She was tired but happy to see me. We spent the night at a motel within walking distance to the clinic. This place was especially tailored and convenient for families of patients. The next day, I'd get to see my dad. He always managed a smile, but a crooked smile was a result of the tumor. I hugged my dad the best I could while he lay in his hospital bed. He would never want us to worry. After the three of us spent some time together, Dad became very tired so mom asked me to go with her to the chapel to pray. It was St. Mary's Chapel, beautiful and reverent. We held hands and prayed for dad and the doctors. It was a surreal moment, a very anxious and scary time for all of us!

The next day, mom and I had a scheduled meeting with Dad's doctor. I remember the setting as if it were today. Mom and I were sitting apart in this small room as there were no two chairs sitting side by side. The doctor walked in wearing a long white jacket. He was very serious as he began to explain to us the extent of Dad's illness. He said they found an astrocytoma brain tumor, which is one of the fastest growing tumors. Dad's tumor was in a location where they couldn't operate. After a moment of pause, I asked the doctor how long Dad had. Before he responded to me, he looked at mom to be sure she wanted to know the answer. She nodded her head. The doctor said Dad had 6-9 months to live. Mayo Clinic is known for their ability to handle patients with severe medical needs, but there was nothing they could do for my dad.

We chose not to tell Dad his prognosis, and as I recall, he never asked. The doctor at Mayo told mom and I that if people don't ask, they don't want to know. Once we got Dad back home, it was a matter of bringing in Home Health Care workers. Dad would eventually lose the ability to walk and eat on his own. He was paralyzed on his right side. Fortunately he was left handed. Dad never had unmanageable pain. I thank God for this mercy! The medications had side affects that gave him nightmares and visions. He was confined to a hospital bed in the living room of his home. Mom had the bed positioned so Dad could see outside their big picture window which faced the street. He could at least see some activity. Being in his own home was the best possible place he could be.

The only way mom survived those nine months was with the help of church friends, family and neighbors. It wasn't uncommon for mom to call a neighbor to come over after dad slipped out of her arms onto the floor. With his paralysis he wasn't able to help her in any way. Our family will forever be indebted to the many people who sat for hours by Dad's side so mom could work, run errands and have a little sanity time.

Dad was 65 on February 5, 1988. He had just retired when he was diagnosed. Life isn't always fair! He would live just nine months until that November. On Dad's last night on this earth my brother Danny and I sat by his side until he passed. We would do the same for our mom when she passed. My dad had many good qualities. He worked hard, could talk to anyone, never met a stranger. He would laugh at his own jokes and he had many. He knew how to play a little bit of everything, like the guitar, trumpet, spoons, harmonica, bugle, and he sang in the church choir. He taught Sunday school and served in many ways. His hobbies were coin collecting, gardening, photography and golf. He loved to take the garden hose and spray a mist of water on a rose and take a photo of it. He had a good eye for photography. My parents weren't perfect, they both had their downside.

One thing I know for sure is that my parents loved us kids and each other. Through thick and thin, they stayed the course. When my parents were about to celebrate their 40th wedding anniversary, we siblings decided to throw them a party. I remember us distinctly saying 10 years is a long time to wait and a lot can happen. Most people wait to have a big celebration on their 50th wedding anniversary, but something told us to do it at their 40th. They never made it to 50 years. We are so grateful for God's prompting in that situation.

Steadfast is the word I chose for this chapter because when Dad accepted Christ as his personal savior, he was a changed man. He never wavered in his faith. He knew his purpose in life was to reach the lost. He read the Bible and knew it well. He would bring homeless people to our home, feed them, let them bathe and give them clean clothes to wear. I love my dad for his selflessness in giving to others.

CHAPTER 14

MY GRACIOUS MOM

Mom was a great listener! It wasn't unusual for us to sit at the kitchen table late at night just talking. She invested in my life! She cared about me and my friends. She always made our friends feel welcome. My mom will forever be a precious memory! She was a prayer warrior for many people, especially our family. I'm sure her prayers became my angels at times. God knew I needed a lot of angels to protect me.

Maybe it's a downfall, or maybe not, I guess it depends on whether you like a clean house or not; but my mom was a perfectionist! My friends loved to come to our house just to mess it up, like throw the pillows off the couch, dirty up a few dishes. I have many great memories of my mom. We played tennis together and traveled to Florida over spring break, just the two of us. As I reflect back on that trip, again, it was such a wise move on mom's part. She took that trip to connect with me. At another time, she drove my friends and I to the Michigan State Dunes in her convertible so we could spend the day at the beach. She loved the sun and would get the most beautiful tan!

When mom was in her forties she nearly died from hysterectomy complications. She lost so much blood that she broke the record at the hospital for pints of blood needed in a short time and also the doctor's record for number of surgeries in a short time. She was so bad one night that the hospital called and told my dad he needed to get there right away. He took Danny with him, but not me. Maybe I was too young, but it made me feel sad and left out. Because mom always got such a great tan, we told her that maybe she got a dark skinned person's blood during all those transfusions and that's why she'd get so tan in the summer. We thank God for all the blood donors!

My mom didn't have hobbies, but she loved to shop and go out to lunch with her friends. What can I say, the apple doesn't fall far from the tree. Nothing brought mom more joy than having her children and grandchildren over for a meal. Mom could make the simplest meal taste so good. She and my dad loved having our sons spend the night. She read to them, played games with them and helped them make cookies. She loved all of her grandchildren.

When mom was younger, she taught Sunday school to preschoolers. She loved reading bible stories and doing simple crafts with those little children. She would give them hugs and treat them just like they were her own. My mom was a warm and loving person, a beacon in my life. She also loved a good basketball game. She could cheer as loud as anyone. Oh Mom, I sure miss you!

One of my biggest regrets was when I was 16 and I embarrassed my mom at the police station. Being at the police station is embarrassment enough. It was in the wee hours of the morning and at the time it seemed so innocent. My friend, Ivy, invited me to spend the night at her older sister's place. She lived close to downtown. Her sister Marilyn and I sat up talking, Ivy had fallen asleep. Marilyn and I weren't tired, so we decided to drive to a local coffee shop that was open 24/7. It was about 1:00 am in the morning. On our way to the coffee shop we got pulled over by a cop for having a loud muffler. What?! Are you kidding me? Once the cop saw I was only 16 and Marilyn was 21 we were taken to the police station. Marilyn got put in jail for the night and fined for having a minor out after midnight. The cops called my mom. When she showed up at the station I was very disrespectful. I'm sure it was my way of saving face. It's a night I'd like to forget.

After Dad's death in 1988, Mom had a lot of decisions to make. Thankfully, her home was paid for and she had all she needed, except Dad. As time went on, Mom got terribly lonely as nothing could fill the void that Dad left in her life. After a few years, she remarried. She met John through a family friend. John had also lost his wife from cancer. Mom and John were married over 20 years when she passed away in 2010. John took good care of my mom and we will always be grateful for that.

In 2006, my mom was diagnosed with stage 4 ovarian cancer. She went through chemotherapy and lost her thick beautiful hair. She always dressed well and took good care of herself, except for excessive sun tanning. But no one was going to rob her of that joy! Even through cancer, my parents were strong. They knew they were going to heaven, their long awaited home.

On social media, I often see the phrase R.I.P., when someone passes away. According to the Bible, not every one who dies will rest in peace, only those who have put their faith and trust in Jesus.

The Bible says in 1 John 1:8-9, "If we claim to have no sin, we are only fooling ourselves and not living in truth. But if we confess our sins to him, he is faithful and just to forgive us our sins and to cleanse us of all unrighteousness."

I know, without a doubt, I'll see my parents in heaven.

Thank you Mom and Dad for
choosing Jesus!

CHAPTER 15

HER LAST DAYS

I remember my mom's final days as if they were yesterday. One month before she passed, I stopped by Mom's on my way home from work to drop off some clothes she had asked me to wash. Mom had just gotten her bath from hospice. She was all dressed. Her hair was starting to grow back and it looked cute, kinda spiky on top. Mom always managed to look stylish even at a time like that.

I spent the next hour helping Mom and John sort through papers to decide what they would need to keep for the coming year. I hope I helped them make good decisions.

A week later, I took a half day vacation to run errands and get caught up on some things at home. That night, our son Jason, daughter-in-law Rachael and, our granddaughter Haley all came over to Mom's for dinner. Duane, Ben and Kathy (Rachael's mom) came too. Kathy had called me earlier to see if she could come to see Mom. Kathy and I had known each other since kindergarten. She wanted to redeem herself for all the times she came over, as a teenager, to help mess up my mom's perfect house. She also wanted to reminisce with my mom in case she wouldn't get to see her again. We all knew Mom was in her final days.

Haley was three, and so excited to be with everybody! John got out the toys and entertained her. She was still a little afraid of mom, as she wasn't sure what to think about her illness. Haley looked at the red spots on my mom's legs and wondered what they were. She gently touched them, and I'm so glad Mom didn't jump, because it would have scared the bageebers out of Haley. We all had a nice and meaningful evening.

On January 18, 2010, John and I took Mom to a local Italian Restaurant for dinner. She wanted to get out of the house even though it took all her energy just to walk in and sit down. We had a very nice dinner, but it was hard to watch mom eat. She couldn't see her food as her eyes had changed, and her finger tips were numb from the treatments. It was difficult for her to hold utensils.

It was a comfort and relief to get her back home. After Mom went to bed that night, John and I talked. His love for Mom was admirable. His heart was breaking as the reality of her loss drew nearer. He feared the future and didn't want to be alone without her. John said, "I can be with a lot of people, but if she's not there, I'm alone, and I don't want to be alone."

I stayed with mom and John for two weeks. I would go to work, then return to their house to fix dinner and help where I could. Mom still had the $100 bill that Duane and I gave her for Christmas in 2008. We gave them another $100 in 2009. I asked mom, what she was saving the money for. She said she wanted a new coat. My sister, Diana, and I would've taken her shopping but she was far too weak. She really didn't need another coat anyway, as she later confessed. I suggested to Mom that she get a manicure instead, and she agreed. So on Saturday, January 23, Diana and I took her to Absolutely Fabulous for a manicure. I chose the color pink without giving much thought to the fact that it would match her funeral dress perfectly. It was this day, January 23, that we would realize just how weak Mom was. She would never go out for fun again.

I went to work that Monday and Tuesday and each day she declined consistently. Then, on Wednesday, I went into work for just two hours to finish some orders. My boss approved three personal days so I didn't need to use anymore vacation time. I wouldn't return to work until after Mom's funeral.

January 28th, was our 38th wedding anniversary. It came and went. Duane bought me yellow roses and a smiley face balloon. It was much needed! I stayed with Mom and John again. We got a hospital bed that week and put it in the front room. Mom would no longer use the bathroom. Instead she would use a portable potty that was next to her bed.

On Friday, January 29th, she took a significant turn for the worse. She was sleeping nearly 24/7. Her speech was slurred and confused. She would sleep with her eyes open which made John frantic! We tried once that Friday, to move her from the bed to the toilet, but her legs collapsed. We would no longer be able to get her up out of bed. John had already lost so much sleep. I had him stay in his bed and I slept on the couch for the next two nights to give him a break. She was now bedridden. I tried my best to help her on the bed pan, but it was all I could do to roll her over. John had already injured his shoulder and was in significant pain.

Many others reached out and offered a helping hand during the daytime, but the evenings were difficult. Early Saturday morning, at about 5:30 am, we called hospice to have her transported to the Hospice House. The ambulance took her on a very cold morning. Mom was surprising alert and talking, so much so, that the nurses at the Hospice Center, checked her in as "active and good".

It wasn't long until she couldn't swallow. The most she had to eat was a couple bites of oatmeal and she didn't like it. She had loved the strawberry smoothies I had made her, so Gayle, John's daughter, made her one that day.

Danny, my brother, and I stayed with Mom that Saturday night at Hospice House. Even though the Hospice House is a great place, we had to stay on the nurses to better manage Mom's pain. It got severe at the end.

Saturday afternoon, Duane and I sat with one of the nurses and she explained that Ovarian Cancer is one of the most painful cancers. The nurses were always hesitant to give us a time frame for Mom. We all watched her severely decline that day. She was no longer responsive, but we kept communicating to her as though she could hear us.

Mom had her whole family by her side. Sunday afternoon, I went into the four season room at the Hospice House and started putting a small puzzle together to take my mind off things. Pretty soon, we had a table full of people. It was a nice diversion. When I returned to Mom's room I could tell her breathing was a struggle. This would be the second time I'd watch a parent die. I stood by her side. I looked away from her face for just a moment and when I looked back at her, she was no longer breathing normally, she was gasping. I went to get the rest of the family, it would only be a matter of minutes until Mom took her last breath at 4:32 pm on January 31, 2010.

We wept and said our last farewells. Within minutes my body began to reveal weakness from the sleep I had missed and the changed life style of the past several weeks. I would not regret one minute of spending time with mom.

She talked about many things during her illness. She had picked out her casket and the pink dress she wanted to be buried in. She would have been pleased to see how beautiful it all came together. The next few days would be spent preparing for the funeral. Ben and his girlfriend, spent hours preparing the perfect slide show capturing so many moments in Mom's life.

My brother Danny provided the best pictures and contacted all our relatives about Mom's passing. I wrote her obituary for the paper and prepared a eulogy. My sister, Diana, wasn't able to help as much because of her recent surgery. All Mom's grandchildren would be Pall-bearers, except Jason who officiated the funeral. Mom would have been proud of her grandchildren.

Mom had a lot of jewelry and she wasn't sure what to do with it all. With her permission we gave much of it away. We set up a table at the church on the day of her funeral so family and friends could select a piece of her jewelry as a remembrance of her. It was a beautiful expression of love to watch people put something on that day that belonged to Mom. We received so many compliments about that gesture.

February 5, would have been our dad's birthday. Mom died January 31, and was buried February 4. As we were standing by her gravesite, my brother Danny looked up to Heaven and said, "Dad is getting a birthday present today, our mom". Precious!

Mom had lost all her thick beautiful
hair from chemotherapy.
She still looks lovely in her wig.

CHAPTER 16

AS SEASONS CHANGE

Indiana's weather can be unpredictable. We've worn shorts in winter and sweatshirts in summer. In spring, we welcome the colorful budding flowers after a cold wet winter. Summer brings sunshine and outdoor activities. Our falls in Indiana are beautiful, as leaves turn from green to yellow, orange and red and there's nothing more breathtaking, than the first snowfall. Along with all the beauty, there's also a chance of weather disasters, like tornadoes or snow storms. Life is much the same way. Every phase, every season, growth spurt, challenge, and age group is delivered on its promise, to never be boring. There is something to learn and appreciate from each stage and season. Sometimes we just want life to be a little more boring, don't we?

In 1986, we began a new season in our lives. We built a two-story home to give us more room for our growing sons. This new neighborhood brought new opportunities. We lived there for 17 years. Do you ever look back and wonder how you made it through those really expensive years? The years full of sports camps, cars and college.

We did what we could to save wisely and remain faithful with our giving. It wasn't easy. Some months we gave more by volunteering our time than giving financially. We did our best. We may waiver in what we do, but God is always faithful. We can never out give the Lord! Proverbs 3:9-10 says, "Honor the Lord with your wealth and with the best part of everything you produce. Then he will fill your barns with grain, and your vats will overflow with good wine". NLT

During those years the theme for our family was sports. We loved football and basketball! We watched Jason play the safety position for the Concord Minutemen every Friday night. Through rain, snow and cold, we were there to sit on those numbing hard bleachers with our half time popcorn and hot chocolate. Jason loved the game and everything about it. His team had many good seasons, but in his senior year they lost every game. UGH!

At the end of the season, there was a fall sports banquet for players and their parents. This is the time coaches give out awards. At the senior sports banquet Jason won the Mental Attitude Award, chosen by his teammates. As I sat there, I could almost feel my heart warm up. We must have been the proudest parents in the room!

Through the years we had watched this guy cheer, yell and run around the house like a crazy man, rooting for his favorite team. He had wall to wall papers in his bedroom with every statistic you could imagine. He knew the names of every player and the plays for his favorite teams. He knew more than the referee, just ask him. But God knew where his passion would lead him.

Then there was basketball. We Hoosiers love our basketball! Season after season we would watch our Concord High School Minutemen! CHS was a perfect fit for passionate basketball fans! The loud music, flashing lights and ecstatic fans made it a great place to be. We'd all dress in our green and white shirts and head for the gym. Did I say green and white? Jason and his friend Troy were very superstitious, so much so, that they both wore a certain favorite shirt to each game. There wasn't anything special about their shirts except that Concord had won when they wore them the first time, so they kept wearing the same shirts and the team kept winning! It worked!

In 1988, when Jason was 14 and Ben 11, Concord played in the State Championship Basketball game in Indianapolis, IN. Shawn Kemp, a senior at the time, went on to play in the NBA. Although Shawn and the team fell short to Muncie Central, it was a year we would never forget. Those were some of Concord's finest years in basketball.

After playing four years of high school football, Jason went on to play his freshman year at Anderson University. That year the AU Ravens, went undefeated, what a contrast from his senior year in high school. On game days, Duane and I would travel 2 1/2 hours each way to watch him play, then take him out for a nice dinner. You've gotta keep those football players fed! This was our time to catch up and see how our son was doing.

In the summer between his freshman and sophomore years of college, Jason went on a mission trip that would change the course of his life. He told us that summer that he wouldn't be returning to Anderson. He had decided to transfer to Bethel College in Mishawaka, IN, just 30 minutes from our home, to study ministry. This change would create a new path for him.

CHAPTER 17

REFLECTING

When both boys were off to college, life seemed to lose its pizazz! The previous season of our life was just a memory. Looking back I'm not sure how we got out of that fog, but we did. I've heard it said, "When your down, just keep putting one foot in front of the other until you figure it out," and we did.

All the years of coaching soccer teams and little league games were a mere blur. Our garage used to be lined with basketball shoes, baseball cleats, football cleats, basketballs, footballs, baseballs and soccer balls. Duane helped them pick out their first car and taught them how to drive. After high school graduation, he built dorm lofts, packed and moved them out of state and sat on enough bleachers to last a lifetime. Duane gave them opportunities he never had. Our best memories were between diapers and graduations. There wasn't a season we didn't enjoy, but don't get me wrong, some were more enjoyable than others.

Being a tomboy growing up paid off for me. I loved shooting baskets or rebounding the ball for Jason and Ben. During baseball season, I would practice playing catch with Ben in the backyard. He could throw a mean pitch leaving my hand burning red. Sometimes he'd throw the pitch so hard, I'd throw the mitt off my hand and clench it with the other. He would just smile as if he was rather proud of himself.

It was fun watching the boys grow up. It was also hard when they were gone.

We loved our family vacations! Duane needed to get away from the heat and pressure of piece work. Piece work is when you get paid for output. The more output the more you get paid. He buffed saxophones in a dingy, hot and dirty factory up to 56 hours a week. When it came time for vacation, we pulled out all the stops so we could get away and have some fun. We got out of Dodge!

When the boys were 8 and 11, we flew to Washington State to visit Duane's brother, Bill and his family. Republic Airlines was running a special with Chex cereal. If you bought 10 boxes of Chex cereal, your child could fly for free. We went to the store and bought 20 boxes of Chex cereal. It was a great time and what a deal! The only way we like Chex cereals is in those yummy Christmas mixes.

Some of our most memorable vacations were those with imperfections. While camping by beautiful Virginia Beach, the cable snapped on our pop up camper and we couldn't open it. All our clothes and food were inside. What happens when something goes wrong? You go to plan B. We located the nearest Sears store and bought the largest tent we could find. We finished our trip by setting the tent up next to our broken camper.

I'm sure our camping neighbors wondered why we were sleeping in a tent when we had a camper sitting next to us. Unbeknownst to us, the campground was next to a naval air station where jets were flying overhead out and back to aircraft carriers for training purposes. This always happened early in the morning. No alarm needed! We laughed at all the calamity!

One evening while we were at the Virginia Beach campground we made spaghetti. I made the sauce and Duane cooked the noodles. As he was draining the water off the spaghetti, the lid slipped out of his hand, and all the spaghetti ended up on the ground. I'll never forget the look on his face. There goes our dinner! He actually tried to scrape the noodles off the ground and back into the pot. I'm still laughing.

Nothing could beat our family time around the campfire. Chilly nights, starry skies, the sound of crackling fire wood and roasting marshmallows. When we all got too cold and tired we would resort to our cozy camper. Each one curling up in his own warm sleeping bag. Those were the good old days when the boys seemed more compatible.

One year we all went to Colorado with Duane's family, and took a rafting trip down the Colorado River. That was fun! The picture of that rafting trip is still posted on a wall in our basement. Photos can easily remind us of where we've been and how much fun we've had.

When we look back, Duane and I are so grateful for all the people who invested in our sons. My parents were great about checking in with the boys and supporting their activities. My mom was their biggest prayer warrior. Youth pastors, Terry Bley and Len Morris, invested a lot of time in their lives. High school coaches like Tim Dawson and Ron

Dietz were good mentors for our sons. Someone once said it takes a village to raise a child. As parents we just need to be sure our children are living in a safe and healthy village. As parents, there are so many firsts. Step by step, prayer by prayer, and through trial and error, we find our way, then we try to help our children do the same.

CHAPTER 18

GOD ONLY KNEW

Shortly after college Jason accepted a job as a youth pastor in a large church close to home. That is where he met his wife, Rachael. She was one of the college students helping out as a volunteer. Anyone who can love and work with junior high students, ranks high on my list.

I was surprised, to say the least, that Rachael was the daughter of my best friend in high school. How could that be? Her mom, Kathy, and I had known each other since kindergarten, but after high school we lost touch for over 20 years. When Jason said he was having a date with her daughter, I think I got a whip lash. All I could think about at that moment was what Kathy and I were like in high school and that was enough to scare me. Once I met Rachael, it was easy to see why he was attracted to her. They were a perfect fit for one another.

After dating nine months, Jason proposed to Rachael at Warren Dunes State Park on Lake Michigan. Rachael loves the sun and beach so it was a perfect place to propose. Almost! According to Pure Michigan, the rugged dune formation rises 260 feet above the lake. His preparation for this day included driving over 100 miles to the Cheesecake Factory in Chicago, IL to get a slice of Rachael's favorite cheesecake. He put her engagement ring inside the cheesecake box. Now picture this, it's a fairly warm summer day and your plan is to carry the ring and cheesecake box up the hill in a small cooler. However, once you get to the top you realize you've forgotten the cooler. So back down you go 260 feet in hot sand… I know his feet were burning. It's funny to even think about how tired he must have been when he finally arrived with everything he needed to propose. In the meantime, Rachael is sunbathing at the top of the dune waiting on her Prince Charming. Every good memory deserves a good story behind it. Rachael said yes and hopefully was able to enjoy her priceless piece of cheesecake.

On May 11, 2002, Jason and Rachael were married. It was a rainy day outside, but the wedding was beautiful! Kathy and I had now caught up like old friends and were just amazed at how God had brought our lives back together after so many years. God knew as Kathy and I were walking to grade school together that someday our children would marry one another, we would share grandchildren, and our moms would die just three months apart. Only God!

The mom's!
We've known each other since kindergarten.

CHAPTER 19

HE IS FAITHFUL

Just days before Jason and Rachael's wedding, Jason became a licensed pastor and earned his Masters of Ministry degree from Bethel College. It was a very eventful week leading up to the wedding. As newly weds, Jason and Rachael went on mission trips. They share a passion for young people. Jason was on staff at the same church for 16 years, while Rachael was teaching elementary school. After four years, they had their first child, Haley Elizabeth. She was born on December 13, with blond hair and blue eyes. And at age 15 she still looks like her daddy. We have enjoyed Haley! Becoming a grandma is the most rewarding second chance a mom can get.

In 2015 Rachael was diagnosed with breast cancer. It was shocking at her young age and with no family history. We went to the Goshen Retreat Women's Health Center the day she had her biopsy. I sat in the waiting room praying for good results. When they found it was cancer, Rachael made the difficult decision to have a double mastectomy. She didn't want to take any chances of it coming back. It was a hard time for them, but God gave them strength and hope. We don't always get what we pray for. God is still faithful!

The GPS changed directions again. If I had to redefine GPS, it would stand for God's Perfect Strategy. In 2016, Jason felt God calling his career in a new direction. He kept his eyes open to opportunities outside of church ministry. It wasn't long before he read about a non-profit organization near Atlanta, GA called NG3 (Next Generation). The job description was right up his ally!

He inquired about it and set up an appointment for he and Rachael to meet with the staff. Jon Stinchcomb, a former player for the New Orlean Saints, was on staff and offered to let them stay in his guest house for the visit. Jason's original plan after high school was to teach history and coach sports. I'm a firm believer that God has a plan for our lives, Jeremiah 29:11. He desires to use our passions on His terms. God took Jason's passion for sports and his love for helping young people and gave him a position with NG3.

When Jason and Rachael quit their jobs to move to Georgia, they were trusting God for His provision. When you work for a non-profit organization, you rely on contributions. It's very humbling and risky, especially when you have a family to support. Rachael was offered a 4th grade teaching position at Lovin Elementary. They needed this steady and reliable income.

They sold their home in Indiana and moved to Loganville, GA. Good ole dad drove the U-Haul truck with all their belongings so they could each drive their own cars. Moving is difficult in many ways, but this move was harder yet because there were so many uncertainties. They were fortunate to find a lovely three bedroom home in a nice neighborhood. Rachael has made all of their homes warm and welcoming and their Georgia home was no exception. Jason worked many hours connecting with students and staff at George Walton Academy. He loved it!

After only one year in Georgia, God opened a door for them to start NG3 back in Indiana. It was like a revolving door. Jason is an organizer! With the knowledge and experience he gained in Georgia, it was a welcoming decision to return to Indiana. We were thrilled!

Jason and Rachael had made many new friends and strong connections in their year in Georgia. Although returning home had it's advantages, it was a year of emotional highs and lows. Saying goodbye is never easy to say, to old friends or new friends.

I sometimes wonder, if the move to Georgia was a testing of their faith. God only knows. Faith is walking where we cannot see and trusting what we do not know. Faith is sometimes following one open door after another. It's unpredictable and sometimes costly, but faith in God is always worth it!

Today, Jason is Director of NG3 in Indiana. This hasn't been an easy walk for them, but God has been ever present. The vision of NG3 is to facilitate character development and small group mentoring in local schools. NG3 stands for Next Generation 3. The 3 represents Character Development, Community service and bringing positive change. NG3 has been a good fit for Jason's skills and passion.

Upon their return from Georgia, Prairie View Elementary gave Rachael her teaching position back. God is so good! Life is often full of uncertainties and challenges! My granddaughters will tell you that every chance I get I say, "It's gonna be a good day!" Sometimes I say it in the afternoon, or even at night, and they'll remind me that the day is almost over. Nevertheless, I hope to leave them with the notion that there is good in every day.

The Bible says in Deuteronomy 31:6-8, "Be strong and courageous. Do not fear or be in dread of them, for it is the LORD your God who goes with you… It is the LORD who goes before you. He will be with you; he will not leave you or forsake you, do not fear or be dismayed."

Jason and Rachael
We admire their faith!

CHAPTER 20

OFF ROAD EXPERIENCE

I have a poor sense of direction, so a GPS is my friend. When setting up the GPS in my car, it gives me options. It asks me if I want to avoid toll roads, difficult intersections, choose the fastest route or the shortest distance. Once the system is set, it will use that same setting over and over again until I change it. My preference is to take the scenic route, but it doesn't give me that option, and honestly the scenic route isn't always practical or the best choice. I've taken the scenic route more than I'd like to admit.

The parallel is that sometimes we're going down the road of life, and we think we're doing just fine, until we realize, we're not where we intended to end up. The worst feeling is when someone is trustingly following you. I know that sinking feeling far too well! I'd be driving along, turning right, then left, going straight for a while and then the hum comes. Hummmm… this doesn't look right! Then, I look in the rear view mirror, and I am humbly reminded it's not just me that's lost, but the one who's following me. It's a bad feeling!

They say, that men have a harder time asking for directions, but I think, we all have a tendency to want to do life alone. We fear looking weak or ignorant. I love the Bible story about the disciples. Here they are standing in the water fishing away, minding their own business, and Jesus walks up and asks them to drop their nets and follow him. Talk about an off road experience. I would've loved to have been in the shadows of Peter and Andrew. Jesus still calls us to follow him. No GPS needed. Just trust! The road might get bumpy at times and it may take longer to arrive than we had hoped, but God always knows the best route for your life and mine. Stress would diminish if we would just trust His plan.

Our youngest son, Ben, prefers an off road experience. He was baptized in India while on a mission trip. How cool is that! He saw first hand the poverty that so many children experience around the world. We're so proud of him for taking this trip. Poverty is hard to see, yet in the presence of so little, these children seem happy. When you give them a stone they create a game. We can learn a lot from them about contentment.

Ben has given us many good memories! In high school he played football and basketball all four years. Fall and winter weekends were spent at games, and we loved it. The camaraderie among fans made sitting on bleachers worth every minute. Ben played hard, and sometimes it came with a cost. He had several sprained ankles and a night at the ER for a concussion. In his senior year, he won the mental attitude award in football. That award meant far more to us then all the points scored or yardage gained. It said a lot about his character. He made us proud!

He was a scrapper on the basketball court! At the forward position he would often get the pass under the basket for a quick two points. Duane and I would sit in the stands and keep score, his score. He'd shoot up a 3 pointer, swish! We'd look at each other, just to compare notes, "How many points does he have now?" There was never a time when we weren't proud of our sons. They played hard, but more importantly, they were good sportsmen.

After high school, Ben decided to play football, for the Anderson University Ravens, a NCAA Division III football team. Before the season started we got a call from him saying he had broken his nose playing touch football in front of his dorm. Another student had jumped in front of him, to intercept a pass, and hit Ben right in the nose. Our hearts sank! If breaking his nose wasn't painful enough, he had to endure the look on his coach's face. Let's just say, his coach wasn't happy with this new freshman, and the injury cost him some playing time.

When we arrived on campus to see him, we couldn't believe this was our son! The break was bad! Surgery was scheduled at a nearby Catholic Hospital. We arranged for him and I to stay in a bed and breakfast near the school so he could have a quiet place to recover. It wasn't long until he was back on the field. After three years and several coaching changes, he decided to forego playing his senior year. As much as we loved watching him play football, we were relieved he was done.

Ben graduated from AU with a Marketing Degree. He lived and worked in Indianapolis for several years. He rented a room from a wealthy widow who enjoyed helping out young people. She would rent them a room in her home in exchange for help around the house. He saved enough money to make a down payment on his first home.

He purchased a house in Indianapolis that was built in the early 1900s. It was a two-story with plenty of room for a single guy. The green shingles on the outside reminded me of my grandmother's home. The front porch extended the length of the house and would be a nice place to relax with a cup of coffee. I was thinking ahead! Like many other homes in this era, it had elaborate wood working around the windows, doors and staircase. The prior owner had trashed the house, so it was going to take a lot of hard work to restore it. Ben saw the potential, and we admired him for that. It took Duane and I awhile to get on board with it. All we could see was costly repairs and it felt overwhelming.

The basement looked like what you'd expect from the early 1900's. The low ceilings made the spider webs that much closer to my head and I don't like spiders! It's one of those places you hope the light bulb doesn't burn out before you make it back to the top of the stairs. Every time I'd go down there I'd stop and look around to be sure there weren't any creepy crawly things peaking out. I was ready to make a mad dash up those stairs.

When the renovating was done, we were one of the first to see it. It looked remarkable! It was transformed throughout with new light fixtures, refinished floors, updated bathrooms and the house was totally repainted. The staircase particularly caught our eye, it had a keen shine to it and led to the bedrooms upstairs. In the morning, Duane started down those shiny stairs in his stocking feet and hit the slippery steps with a bumpity bump, bump! His back side was bruised, but we knew he was going to be okay. We all had a good laugh about it. Little did we know that Ben had used furniture polish to clean the stairs. He's a guy! Big smile from mom!

Spiritual Application: God always sees the potential. He can fix what's broken. After all He was a carpenter.

These beautiful Indian children are showing their love to Ben

The house Ben renovated in Indianapolis

CHAPTER 21

WESTWARD BOUND

In 2011 Ben had an opportunity to move out west. He longed to see and experience more than Indiana could offer. Who could blame him? We were sad to see him go, but we have always wanted our sons to be free to do their own thing. As we watched him drive away for that 2500 mile road trip, Duane and I both had a lump in our throat and a tug on our heart. This move was different, as we couldn't just jump in the car and drive a couple hours to see him.

Once Ben was settled into his own place, we flew out to Oregon for our first time visit. This would be a new experience for us. Ben's apartment was within walking distance to eateries, stores and coffee shops. It was much faster to walk than to try to find a parking spot on the narrow streets. Everyone we passed on the sidewalk seemed friendly and many people were out walking their dogs. We love dogs! Portland was a fun experience!

A common bumper sticker might read, "Keep Portland Weird". There are many reasons for the nickname, but for me it surely has to do with the yearly Buck Naked Moon Ride. Yup, it's just like it sounds. Ben assured us that he's weird to them too, because he's so normal. That was good news to me!

Ben was a great tour guide. He hit the main attractions that he thought we would enjoy. The Multnomah Falls on the Columbia River Gorge, was powerful and breathtaking. The peacefulness and beauty of the Japanese Gardens made me want to linger. I could spend hours in a garden like that! Just give me a bench, a cup of chai and I'll sit and savor the beauty. We attended church together and met some of his friends. A quote I found by Yogananda was worth capturing. "Those who live passionately, teach us how to love. Those who love passionately, teach us how to live." How true!

At the time of our visit, Ben was working for Nike. Later on he accepted a job at Adidas headquarters in Portland. Their international headquarters are located in Herogenaurach, Germany. In 2016 Adidias sent Ben to Germany for three months. With Duane being a lover of history, we decided to make the trip while Ben was there. It seemed like the perfect time. It gave Duane a chance to check off several boxes on his "bucket list" while spending time with our son. We flew into Berlin and then on to Nuremberg where we would stay for about two weeks.

We took a winding bus ride up Germany's steepest road. It was 6000 feet high to the top of Obersakzberg mountain where we toured the well known Eagle's Nest, an estate that Hitler was given as a 50th birthday present. Evil describes Adolf Hitler, a man who showed the world what the dark side of dictatorship looks like. We rode in the gold plated elevator that is still in tact, just as it was when Hitler was alive. In the end, Hitler was a coward! He took his own life so he wouldn't have to stand trial for the thousands of innocent lives he destroyed.

We toured the Concentration Camp in Munich. This landmark is hard to see, as it reminds us of all the wrongs done to the Jewish people. We saw the wired fence around the camp where many men would try to escape. They knew they would be shot before getting over the fence but they had lost all hope. We visited the court house where they held the Nuremberg trials. It was a great history lesson and a trip we'll never forget.

In Germany we walked on historical brick streets lined with huge cathedrals fashioned with stained glass windows and large wooden and iron doors. Early one morning, as we walked around the square to do some sightseeing, we found a bench by a tree to sit on. We sat and talked until we decided to take in a few of the local shops. When we got into one of the stores, Duane realized he didn't have his cell phone. We began to backtrack to the area of the bench. In the distance, we saw a man who noticed us walking toward him and he held up the phone. Worry or panic must have been written all over our faces as he recognized us frantic Americans. The man kindly returned the phone and all we could say was how grateful we were to him.

We visited Salzburg Austria just on the border of Germany. We toured the film location for the Sound of Music. It did not disappoint! The terrain is highly mountainous, due to the presence of the Alps. It truly is a place where the hills come alive!

CHAPTER 22

HEARTBREAK THEN JOY

If I were to identify the saddest day of my life, it would be a day in the summer of 2009, when we learned that doctors couldn't find a heartbeat for our second granddaughter, Aleigha Grace. Rachael was seven months along in her pregnancy. Duane and my grief multiplied knowing the loss and heartache our son and daughter-in-law would bear. There are no words to console someone whose pain is so deep!

The evening I learned about Aleigha, I was at a nursing home visiting my Uncle Carl Miller, who was terminally ill with cancer. My Aunt Eleanor and I were having a nice visit in his room when I got a call to come home. During the same time that my Uncle Carl was sick, my mom was going through treatment for stage 4 Ovarian cancer.

When my cell phone rang, Duane told me I needed to come home right away, but he wouldn't say why. A million thoughts went through my head! The sound of his voice told me it was serious. On my way home, I prayed! Was it my mom, one of the kids, or could it be the baby? When I walked in the house, Duane met me with these words, "They lost the baby." Those crushing words filled every ounce of my being with brokenness. I could hardly breathe! We jumped in the car and went to Jason and Rachael's where her mom, Kathy, had already arrived.

Kathy read from Psalms 139, the most comforting words! We cried and cried as we shared our grief mostly in silence and tears. If it weren't for being a believer, I'm not sure how we would have handled our loss. Jason and Rachael are the kind of couple that have tried to do everything right. They followed Jesus faithfully and yet in 2009 God allowed their hearts to be shattered, but only for a while. The Psalmist wrote in chapter 30 that weeping may stay for the night but joy comes in the morning. God knew!

A few days later when they held Aleigha's funeral outside, it was a lovely, but breezy day. The morning of her funeral I had to decide what to wear. What does a grandma wear to her baby granddaughter's funeral? For some reason that day, I made a choice to wear a red and white summer dress. Even with a broken heart, I wanted her little life to like the color of my dress. Sadness was everywhere and for that moment I wanted to choose something colorful in the midst of so much darkness. It will be a glorious day, when I see Aleigha in heaven and I'm quite sure she'll like the color red. Aleigha Grace sounds like an angel, don't you think?

The guitarist played songs like Do Lord, and Jesus Loves Me. The Pastor spoke words of encouragement. At the end of the service, when Jason picked up his daughter's small casket and put it on the table, it was all I, as his mother, could do not to breakdown. Tears were everywhere, but so was Jesus! He knew and understood our pain.

There's a gospel song called No one understands like Jesus, written by John W. Peterson. "No one understands like Jesus. He's a friend beyond compare. Meet Him at the throne of mercy, He is waiting for you there. Every woe He sees and feels; tenderly he whispers comfort, and the broken heart he heals. When the days are dark and grim; no one is so near, so dear as Jesus."

After a couple years had passed, Rachael gave birth to their third daughter, a beautiful and healthy little girl, Natalie Kate Thompson. Although I had wished that Natalie would be born on my dad's birthday, February 5, she was born two weeks early on my stepdad's birthday January 21. My mom married John a couple years after my dad passed away. It all made sense that John would enjoy the irony of her being born on his birthday. We found great pleasure in sharing the good news with him.

God knew this baby, this pregnancy was a walk of faith for Jason and Rachael. God granted them grace and mercy along with a wonderful miracle. As I was holding Natalie at three weeks old, and looking at her perfect frame, I knew how much my own mom and dad would've loved to hold her too.

Haley was 4 years old when Natalie was born. She was a gentle and kind sister. On Mother's Day, May 11, 2011, Duane and I went to Natalie's baby dedication service. The Pastor asked all the parents to come up front with their children. As he began to speak, he talked about how many people would touch these new little lives. Haley was sitting in a chair behind us, and shouted real loud, "46!" We couldn't help but laugh knowing big sister was listening to every word and she had her own number of influencers.

CHAPTER 23

CHERISHED MEMORIES

Haley at two was expressive and animated, just like her daddy used to be. She moved her little hands as she talked, to express her excitement. It tickled us so! Her long blond hair was styled in pigtails with bright yellow ribbons. She appeared to dance as she walked.

When Haley was four years old, she asked me, "Grandma when I'm five will you buy me a new doll?" I said, "Well, we'll see." Haley says, "because when I'm 6 I'll still like dolls, and when I'm 7 I'll still like dolls, and when I'm 8, 9, 10, 11, 12 and 40, I'll still like dolls!!" I say, that girl will make a good salesperson someday!

She fixed my hair in a ponytail with clips on each side of my face to hold the loose hairs in place. I was quite a sight to be seen. She said to me, "Grandma, when you get ready to go to a fancy place or a fancy house you come over and let me do your hair." What a hoot! She was feeling pretty good about her hairstyling experience!

When Haley was five she said, "Grandma, what do you think I'll name my husband?" Big smile!

"I'm going to have four children and name them Abby, Tyler, Isabelle, and Keaton!!" At least she has the order right, husband first and kids next.

Haley says to me, "Daddy gets our groceries." I ask her, "Does he do a good job?" She said, "Yes, but he always buys candy." I said, "Is that a good thing?" She says, "Yes, but he needs to get what's on the list first." Hum, I wonder where she heard that? (I'll bet the candy was Twizzlers!)

Haley's favorite stuffed animal was a little white lamb named Lilly. She loved Lilly and would take her every where. It was quite a dreadful day when they thought they might have lost Lilly. Lilly is still around, somewhere, but you won't hardly recognize her limp and stained fur. It's all the result of lots of car rides and cuddles.

Much like her father, Haley enjoys sports. She has a good sense of humor and delights in making people laugh. She's soon to finish her freshman year in high school. I wonder where the time has gone.

At 13 months old Natalie still wasn't ready to walk or crawl, but she scooted everywhere! She would scoot forward and backwards as fast as she could. She earned the nick name "scooter". She finally started to walk at 18 months, but not one day before she was ready.

Natalie is tenderhearted and kind, cautious and sincere. She knows what she likes. She's creative and fun! She loves music and dance, volleyball and basketball. She's a good communicator for an eleven year old. She knows how to ask questions and she tells a story with great detail. She has light brown hair and lovely green eyes.
She looks like her mother.

CHAPTER 24

JOURNAL ENTRIES

Parents and Grandparents, catch it while you can! Kids talk freely when they're young, innocent and uninhibited by social graces. Capture the moments in writing because as much as you think you will, you won't remember it all. As kids grow, their vocabulary increases but the sharing decreases. Write it while you can. These are entries I recorded as dated.

- I was watching Haley and Natalie tonight, 12/11/2011. Haley was in one of her talkative moods. She began telling me about a movie they watched. She said, "Grandma, there was a really old lady in the movie, she must've been 98 degrees."
- Haley and I made snow angels in our backyard - 2012
- Natalie can jabber up a storm. When she doesn't like something she holds her arm straight out and says "stop it"! She's only two.
- Haley calls our whirlpool tub the swirl tub.
- Haley and I went to Cookies and Canvas to paint a duck. While we were painting, Haley leans over and whispers to me, "Grandma this is my first time and I'm doing my very best". AWE! She's only 6.
- We went to Barnes and Nobles in 2013. Haley liked the Doc books, but Natalie liked spinning the book rack.
- Build a Bear is a favorite place! They find a bear, pick out it's clothes, give it a bath and away we go.
- Duane played button-button, Simon says and musical chairs with the girls today. Natalie was awesome! Even

though she didn't fully understand the concept, she laughed whether she won or lost. She just loved to play.

- When Natalie would lead button-button, she would put both her hands behind her back but only bring out the hand with the button in it. Hilarious! Let's admit it, button-button is a confusing game!
- Simba (aka, grandpa) and Haley had a date night when she was 7. They went to see Dolphin Tale, then to Honey's Yogurt for dessert.
- When Natalie was 3 and spending the night I said a prayer with her before she went to sleep. Natalie asked me, "Where is God?" I said, "He's in Heaven". Natalie says. "Why?" I said, "He's preparing a place for us so we can go be with him someday." Natalie, speaking fast and being very anxious says, "I'll have to go home and pack and then come back… mommy and daddy will miss me." I said, "No we're not going there now." Natalie says, "Why? "I said, It's not our time." Precious!
- Haley and I went for a scavenger hunt on a rainy day in our neighborhood. We each listed six things the other person had to see as we took our walk. Things like a bird, a blue car, a wreath… it was Haley's idea. We had so much fun in the rain. We took an umbrella.
- Christmas 2015, Haley wrote her own monologue of what Christmas means to her. There wasn't a dry eye in the house.
- Tonight Haley got a round hair brush stuck and tangled in her hair. It was so bad we finally had to use vegetable oil to get it out. What a mess! We still laugh about the tangled mess.
- While taking a paddle boat ride at Linton Enchanted Garden's, I steered the boat right into the weeds and we

couldn't turn around. We had to call one of the workers over to push the boat around. I think Natalie and Haley were embarrassed.

- We took a road trip with the girls to Noah's Ark and the Creation Museum in Petersburg, Kentucky. It was a great experience to wander through the Garden of Eden and to see history portrayed with such creativity.
- Natalie's first plane ride was to Orlando, FL to visit Disney World in 2018. She looked so cute pulling her little luggage bag through the airport while holding Simba's hand.
- The girls loved playing store. One of us shops and the other handles the money. There were always coupons, so sometimes I would get back more then I spent. Every time I shopped I had to be another person so I made up funny names like Silly Sally Sue. We'd laugh a lot.

The best way for me to show our granddaughters the importance of giving and doing for others, was to have them involved in the process.

- One day, we went to the Dollar Store and bought several gifts, cards and gift bags. The girls selected each card, one for each patient, and they helped select the gifts. Candy was a favorite! Once we purchased the gifts, signed each card with encouraging words, we put them in pretty gift bags. We delivered them to residents at a local Nursing Home. The girls were great! They interacted with the patients. It was quite an experience. Sometimes the uncertainty of a nursing home can be scary, but the girls always made me proud. It gave them a chance to see how a little gesture can make someone happy. We've also taken blankets to the homeless shelter. My prayer is that Haley and Natalie are sensitive to those less fortunate, and that they are willing to help when they can.

Natalie at age 8 says to me, "Grandma, next to my family and God, I love puppies and babies." Awe!!!

- Just recently, Duane took the girls horseback riding on separate days so he could have quality time with each one. He wanted it to be a surprise, so he didn't tell them where they were going. Natalie went first on Tuesday, so Haley tried to get out of Natalie where they went. Natalie wasn't going to have anything to do with revealing the secret, so she told Haley grandpa was taking her fishing. What a hoot! Way to keep a secret Natalie!

There's something special about sharing a laugh with your sister.

CHAPTER 25

EVERYTHING GOES THROUGH DAD

The grand girls are now 15 and 11. At times when we watch the girls, instead of asking us something, they'll text their dad instead. The request is something we could've handled or answered, but they felt more comfortable asking dad. Duane and I chuckle because *everything* has to go through dad.

As I've thought about this, it's such a compliment to Jason. Just to give you an example, the other night I was staying with the girls while Jason and Rachael were at Cleveland Clinic for Rachael's surgery. One night Haley had a friend over for a short time after Natalie was in bed. Haley and her friend were laughing and talking quite loud. Instead of Natalie coming to me in the next room, she texted her dad in Cleveland to have him tell Haley to be quiet. I'm chuckling.

You know why, right? It's because dad get's the job done! The second reason could be that Natalie wanted to be sure that dad knew Haley was being annoying. Big smile!
Isn't this exactly what our heavenly Father wants from us? He delights in our seeking Him out. As Haley and Natalie get out on their own, my prayer is that they will <u>always</u> seek out their Heavenly Father.

"Seek first his kingdom and his righteousness, and all these things will be given to you as well."
Matthew 6:33 NIV

CHAPTER 26

THE JESUS FACTOR

Duane and I have had a good life, but like most couples, we've had our fair share of difficult days. There were times we had to plow through and pray through. When I say, "Plow," I'm thinking of a huge piece of machinery barreling down hard to clear a huge snow pile. As an Indiana Hoosier, we know a lot about snow plows. There's no easy way to get through difficult times. Sometimes it's the work of the Potter (God) and at other times it's the result of our poor choices. During our 50 years of marriage, there were days we just didn't like each other, days when the tension was so thick in our home you could cut it with a knife. In some seasons, it felt like we were oil and water and you know what that looks like. I've heard it said, that if two people are like oil and water they can't exist together. But our God, parted the Red Sea, and that same God took two very different personalities, that resemble oil and water, and made our marriage flourish. We have the Jesus factor in our marriage.

God took our differences and graciously melted them together. We have a great deal of respect and love for one another. It took a lot of self examination and surrendering to the Lordship of Jesus Christ to get us to where we are today. We are beyond grateful!

I've learned many lessons, but perhaps the most impactful one is don't try to fix someone else. Pray and let God do the fixing. Sometimes the one that needs the most fixing may be the one praying. Just saying! When we bow down to His lordship, murky waters become very clear. Remember, Jesus is a carpenter by trade. He can fix stuff and He can fix us!

CHAPTER 27

SHOULD'VE MADE HEADLINES

We've had the privilege to travel many places. We've been to Washington State, California and Oregon. We've traveled as far East as Nantucket Island. We've been North and South and many places in between. We've traveled to Hawaii, Jamaica, Mexico and the Bahamas. We went on an Alaskan Cruise with four other couples for our 25th anniversary. We had the time of our life! We've seen the magnificence of Banff Canada. We explored the history of Germany and Austria. Some of our most amazing vacations have been with family and friends. When you go with someone on vacation it allows you to reminisce those times over and over.

A few years ago, we rented a cabin in Tennessee. We invited my cousin Pam and Dave to go with us. I knew it would be a good time. There was a newly built sky bridge in Gatlinburg, TN with glass floor panels in the middle. Pam was determined to walk across it. It also happens to be the longest pedestrian suspension bridge in North America. Dave and Duane decided to sit it out. They were scaredy cats for sure! Pam and I put on our big girl shoes and took the sky lift to 1800' high where it overlooked the Smokey Mountains. After taking in the sights from atop we looked down below to see our darling husbands waiting for their brave wives to return. Wink! Wink!

As soon as Pam and I stepped on the bridge, we grabbed hold of the rails. All of a sudden, we weren't so brave! The bridge would sway the whole time. Pam was in the lead. I followed at a steady pace behind her. Once we reached the glass panels on the bridge, Pam came to a screeching halt! I'm sure she was just assessing the situation, making sure there weren't any cracks in the glass. Almost like in slow motion she extends her left leg until her foot is over the glass. That a girl, Pam, one step at a time. I was glad she was first. I had already determined to walk as fast as the swaying bridge would let me, but not look down. We crossed to the other side of the glass panels with shaky knees but proud as peacocks. What a great experience, after it was over, of course!

CHAPTER 28

EXPERIENCES OF A LIFETIME

Would you rather have a gift or an experience? Thoughtful gifts will always be cherished. For my 50th birthday, my son, Ben surprised me with a scrapbook crafted by friends, co-workers and family members. Each person designed their own page with fun pictures and memories. I will cherish that album for the rest of my life. Three of my friends from work, that contributed, have since passed away. As I look at their pictures and read their comments it brings back fond memories. I am so sorry they each passed away at such a young age. That scrapbook is a cherished gift.

Our daughter-in-law, Rachael, made me my first photo album. For Duane, she framed pictures of the girls holding letters that spelled out SIMBA, aka Grandpa. Those kind and thoughtful gestures are the kind of gifts with lasting memories. It wasn't something she bought, but something she made, that made it so meaningful. Gifts can last a lifetime, but so can experiences. I love seeing someone's face light up as they reminisce about a happy experience.

Duane has surprised me so many times on my birthday! He's a thorough planner and thoughtful! If truth be known, I don't really like surprises, but he does. We've always tried to do something special for those milestone birthdays. Finding ways to celebrate keeps life fun and exciting, and it doesn't need to break the bank.

On Duane's 40th birthday his brother Bill flew in him from Washington State to surprise him. Bill snuck up behind Duane while he was grilling hamburgers in the backyard of our home. I love the surprised look on Duane's face! What a cherished moment!

On another milestone birthday, Duane flew in a Top Gun WW II fighter War Plane, the kind that does barrel rolls and loops and makes you turn green. He had a grand time! He talked about feeling the g-force and the pressure as the plane went straight up. What an adventure!

For many years I told Duane that I wanted to skydive. He could not picture me skydiving anymore than the man on the moon. Now, think about that for a minute. All Duane could remember is how scared I was of roller coasters. He said, you will never skydive because you don't even like roller coasters. He was right, but he was wrong. Roller coasters no, skydive yes! I had planned it all in my mind. I thought about being in the plane, I thought about jumping out of the plane and in my mind I did it so many times, that doggone it, I was ready!

I asked God to bless and confirm my skydiving plan to jump on Saturday, September 7, 2003. Many days went by without a word from God. On Labor Day, September 1, early in the morning, I'm reading from the last chapter of Secrets of the Vine, by Bruce Wilkinson. On page 119 it says, "Are you standing precariously at a launching point in your life? Do you hear a voice calling? It is the Lord. I hope you jump." Now if that isn't a word of confirmation, I don't know what is.

Finally, for my 50th birthday, he gave me a gift certificate to skydive. In the fall of 2003, I put on a jumpsuit, climbed in the plane and listened to all the instructions. When it came time to scoochie myself up to the door, I knew this was the real deal. I took hold of the open door with one hand and stepped, yes I stepped, out of that plane at 10,000 feet. I was standing on a small step. Once the tandem jumper was positioned on my back they said, "Okay Karen, let go" and off we went into the wild blue yonder. Every moment of that jump was the excitement I knew it would be. I took in every bit of the feeling, the emotions, and the experience without fear. I was prepared!!!! What a ride! Thank you Duane for believing in me!

When Duane turned 60, our sons bought him a gift certificate to drive in the Indy 500. Ha, just kidding! But we headed to Chicagoland Speedway in Joliet, IL, where he participated in an auto race. We watched him climb into the open window of that little car with helmet and jumpsuit in place... I knew he was sweating! He might have been swearing too. He was so cramped in that little race car. When the flag was lifted, the drivers took off but Duane was in SLOW motion. He said he had the pedal to the metal but it wasn't going very fast. For him, it felt like Nascar! Oh my goodness, he was so glad to get out of that little car... but what a thrill of a lifetime!

One of the scariest adventures Duane ever had, was white water rafting on the Gauley River in West VA. He went with a couple friends from our area. Just for a little background, the Gauley River is a 105 mile-long river in West Virginia. It merges with the New River to form the Kanawha River. This is a very popular place to white water raft, but there are always risks. That's why you have to sign your name to a 100 page disclaimer. Slightly exaggerated! The Gauley River has cut a gorge up to 500 feet deep in places. It flows through the gorge for approximately 25 miles with a stream gradient of 28 feet per mile. It can be very dangerous!

On this excursion, the rafting company took two rafts for the number of participants. Duane was in a separate raft than the guys he went with. As they approached one of the rapids, they hit it with such a force that Duane fell out of the raft. On this trip he was knocked out of the raft twice. The second time he went down, he got wedged underneath the raft and couldn't catch his breath or see clearly due to the force of the water. He crashed face first into a large boulder, knocking out his front tooth and bruising his face. The guys in the raft were fiercely trying to find him and pull him back in the raft. Thank God they did!

I've never been one to have a lot of premonitions, but I have had a couple. On the day before Duane came home, I was driving down a street not too far from our house. As clear as the sky is blue, I had Duane's face flash before me and he was missing a tooth. The next morning I walked out of our bathroom after taking a shower, and he was sitting on the edge of our bed. He had just gotten home. He smiled at me and sure enough he was missing his front tooth. I remember saying to him, I knew it! I knew that happened to you. WHOA!!!!

That rafting trip would be his last. He actually felt like he could have lost his life under the raft. When you can't see and you can't breath and there's nothing but rushing water, it's a frightening experience. He had enough rafting for this lifetime.

Duane on his Top Gun flying excursion

Prepared to skydive! Celebrating my 50th birthday

CHAPTER 29

ALASKA

In 2001, we started planning for our 25th wedding anniversary the following year. We decided to invite four couples over for an evening to see if they would want to go on an Alaskan cruise with us to celebrate. Before they left that evening, they were all in. To this day we call ourselves the Alaska Group. The four couples, were Tony and Anne, Bob and Marlene, Gerry and Sue and John and Barb. I mention their names because some of them will be included in this story. We've known these people for decades. They're the kind of friends that show up for every special event in your life and then some.

Duane planned this fabulous cruise! We took a brand new Carnival Cruise Ship. Duane found it online and watched it being built, then delivered to the dock where we would board the ship. Our flights left out of Chicago O'hare Airport. Because of an early morning flight we booked motel rooms for the night before. After everyone arrived at the motel we stood in the hallway talking and preparing for the flight the next day. All of a sudden, Tony says, "I don't have my wallet!". His wife Anne, turns 10 shades of white.... And she said TOOONY you have to have your wallet to fly! Once we realized he wasn't joking, Gerry comes up with a plan. Thank God for quick thinkers! Gerry said, "I'll call Corey and have him meet me at a half way point on the toll road. Corey's a good guy he said, he'll do it." So Anne called

Marcy, her daughter, and tells her, "You need to find dad's wallet at home and give it to Corey so he can bring it to Gerry". This plan worked and generous Gerry, gave Corey a nice tip for meeting him half way. Every day for the rest of our trip the guys would say … "Wallet check", and everyone had to confirm they had their wallet. We laughed about that the entire trip!

This Cruise went down as one of the best experiences of our lives. We flew from Chicago into Anchorage. We stayed overnight in Anchorage, then took the Alaska Railroad Train ride through some of the most scenic places we'd ever seen. We boarded our ship in Resurrection Bay in Seward. Duane and I had a Portside view. Early in the morning we went to the top deck to see the Hubbard Glacier, one of the largest in North America. The Cruise Ship had a formal evening where everyone got dressed up for a lovely dinner and pictures. The guys were all in their suits and ties and us ladies in long gowns. It was a special night!

We stopped at Valdez, Juneau, Skagway and Ketchikan. We saw eagles, whales, sea lions and beautiful glaciers and scenery. John, Barb, Duane and I took a small plane ride as one of our excursions. The pilot weaved the plane in and out of the mountains hoping to let us spot a bear. We never did. He landed the plane on an amazing secluded island where the only sound you could hear was the sound of loons. The scene was breathtaking and peaceful!

CHAPTER 30

THE BLESSINGS OF FRIENDSHIP

Over the years Duane and I have been blessed with faithful friends. Some people walk in and out of our lives and that's okay. Not all friendships are meant to last a lifetime. Some friendships are for a reason, some are for a season and some are for life. In my retirement years, I've become more intentional about bringing people together. Everyone has a story. I love a good story, don't you? I believe most people are willing to share their story if they know we are sincere and want to hear it. In my friendships, we share what's going on in our lives. We laugh together. Sometimes we exchange recipes. It's always nice when food's involved. As trust is built we share the deeper things of life. Sometimes we just sit on a bench in a beautiful garden and appreciate the beauty around us. You know you have a good friend when you are comfortable enough to be quiet and just be! A good friend will lend a helping hand and be there for you without you even having to ask them. While working 33 years at Bayer HealthCare I met some wonderful people and made some amazing friends! There was never a doubt in my mind that God led me to this job.

My sister, Diana, will always be my best friend and confidant. She and I are as different as night and day in many ways. When we were kids, Diana liked dolls and pretty things, and I liked to run and play ball. She is the oldest and I the youngest with our brother Danny in the middle. Diana likes fiction and I like biographies. She can talk circles around me. Her laugh makes me laugh. When she gets to telling a joke or repeating a cartoon story...since she knows the punch line, she'll start laughing so hard I can't understand a word she's saying... but I start laughing because she's laughing. Oh my, what fun! I might never hear the punch line, but we'll still have a good laugh. We both like to shop and hang out together. We enjoy having lunch and a good conversation. One time we were on the toll road and completely missed our exit because we were so engaged in our conversation.

Most importantly, my sister and I share the same faith. Diana has a quiet ministry. I say quiet because she would never want to bring attention to herself, so I will. She types up encouraging words from scripture and puts them on a small piece of paper. There's not a person she encounters throughout the day that doesn't receive a message. I've seen a cashier walk around and give her a hug because those words were exactly what she needed to hear that day. There was a young man bagging her groceries and after reading the message, he asked my sister if she had any more of those messages he could have. I'm proud of you sis! I will cherish and enjoy my sister as long as this life will let us, and then there's Heaven!

My sister, Diana, had the most beautiful auburn hair.

CHAPTER 31

LEARNING TO BE

A few months ago I had an old neighbor come over and help me paint my kitchen table top. We reconnected in the grocery store. That seems to happen a lot for me. In our conversation at the store, she told me she had started her own furniture refinishing business. Because our kitchen table needed a fresh coat of paint, I asked her if I could hire her to paint it. She said, "Yes".

One day while she was painting we had a very interesting conversation. She began to share with me her political position and thoughts about many different topics. As she talked she seemed overwhelmed by all that was going on in the world. At the same time, she told me about all the Podcasts and Blogs she reads or listens to that have inspired her. Her memory is like a sponge, so when she expels her thoughts, there's a lot going on in there. I could see it on her face! I said to her, "Do you find it difficult to just be?" She stared at me for a minute and said, "Yes, I guess so."

Our mind is incredible! Our mind has many functions including our perception, imagination, thinking, intelligence, judgement, language and memory, as well as non cognitive aspects such as emotion and instinct. What we fill our mind with will determine our moods, our opinions, our knowledge, or our lack of such. It's enough to make us pause and evaluate how we feed our minds. There was nothing wrong with what she was expressing and I was honored to hear her genuine concerns.

I was reminded of what David wrote in Psalm 46:10, God says, “Be still, and know that I am God; I will be exalted among the nations, I will be exacted in the earth.” What does “be still” mean in our lingo today? Just be! Chill out! Let go! Relax! During my conversation with this gal, I wanted so badly to say, “STOP listening to the podcast and reading the blogs.” What she was feeding her mind was overwhelming her. My friend isn't that much different then the rest of us. It's so easy to exalt someone else more than God, without even realizing it.

Our minds are amazing, but they can be dangerous. When we feed our bodies healthy food there's a good chance we'll have a strong and healthy body. And if we feed our minds with too many different voices and opinions there's a good chance we'll become confused and restless. A clear mind is a focused and productive mind. When we are bombarded with social media posts, it can become our socialization outlet for surface relationships. Too many times we let social media determine our worth. Even at my age, I too enjoy seeing who likes my post and supports my thoughts. But it becomes dangerous when we allow others to define our worth. God is the only one we can trust to determine our value. Can I get an Amen?

God loves us so much that he sent His only son, Jesus, to die in our place, John 3:16. We won't find another person who will love us that much. We love Him back when we give Him first place in our life.

CHAPTER 32

TOUGH LESSONS

God is our best teacher! He watches me and you for a chance to educate us and teach us life lessons. Many years ago when I was still working, I had the opportunity to travel. It was on a return flight home that has stayed with me. As I was walking down the corridor to my gate in O'Hare Airport, there was a teenage guy with a choker collar, tattoos, and a dowdy look about him. You know what I'm saying. You see someone and you have a thought go through your mind, nice shirt, cute hair, nice shoes, or the more shameful thoughts, the ugly thoughts.... We all have them from time to time. When I saw this young man, I had an ugly thought. As soon as I had that thought God nudged me! I mean, I knew God didn't like my thought and he was going to do something about it.

As I got to the gate, guess what, here comes the guy. I had this awful thought go through my mind, "What if he sits next to me on the plane?" I chuckled to myself thinking, "Now wouldn't that be funny?" I was dressed up because I was on a business trip. I only mention that to point out the distinct difference in our outward appearances. As I got to my aisle seat, close to the front, there was no one sitting in the window seat. I had just gotten comfortable and here comes "the guy". He had his headset on and when he turned his head my way, I knew the seat was his. We barely made eye contact as he sat down. There was no doubt in my mind that

God put him next to me for a reason and I was determined to find out why.

People were still boarding the plane and finding their seats. I looked over at him and introduced myself. He said, "I'm Jody." He took his headset off and for the next hour or so, Jody and I talked the entire time. He was flying into South Bend to meet his aunt, from Michigan. She would be picking him up. He had been in some trouble and was going there to live with her for a while. The details are sketchy to me, but the life lesson is still fresh in my mind. Jody, I've never forgotten his name, and I had a deep and meaningful conversation.

I shared with him those areas of my own life I thought he could relate to. Remember how I mentioned my reckless years? I shared my testimony with him and he was amazingly open and friendly. I had a Christian book with me and I gave it to him as a gift. You had to be there to know how special that hour became to us. It brings tears to my eyes. Jody was a young man who had a very hard life. He was prepared to sit in that seat with his headset on the entire plane ride and never talk. After we landed in South Bend and prepared to depart the plane, I looked back for the first time. It felt like every eye was looking at me and Jody, probably wondering what these two very different people had in common to talk the entire flight. I left that airport and on my ride home I replayed everything that happened from the moment I saw this young man to the time we landed. He told me at the end of the flight that he was surprised by our conversation, and how easy it was for us to talk. He said, "I was just planning on listening to my music." On that day,

God taught me a lesson. Instead of hoping the kid in a choker collar doesn't sit next to me, now I pray he will. God has allowed me to remember his name, so every time I'm reminded of Jody, I say a prayer for him.

In the early 1990s, a co-worker and I were asked to fly to New York to give a presentation to the president of the Diagnostics Division and his group of eight vice presidents. We were well prepared for everything except bad weather. On our way to New York our flight was cancelled a couple times and we nearly gave up and went back home. We finally made it to LaGuardia Airport, only to be told our luggage didn't make all the flight changes. We arrived late at our motel and had to be at the meeting at 9:00 am the next day.

The next morning as we walked into the office outside the conference room, where we were to present, I saw a familiar face. Rosemary, was the Quality Assurance Compliance Manager, that I had met and liked. I explained to her what happened to our luggage and that I didn't have a fresh change of clothes to put on for that day. I said, "Rosemary, what would you do in my situation?" There wasn't much that could be done, but I wanted to see what she would say. She gave me the best advice, she said while she was watching the Miss America Pageant, one of the girls was asked what she would do if the heel on her shoe broke off while she was walking across the stage? The contestant said, "She would kick off her shoes and keep on walking." That was all I needed to hear. I went into the conference room holding my head high and gave it my best shot. These executives couldn't have cared less about what I had on, navy slacks and a white casual top. They had much bigger concerns. We had prepared well, but nothing prepared us for the inconvenience and somewhat embarrassing moment of not having the right attire. When you find yourself in a pinch, or tough situation, remember this story and just kick your shoes off and keep on walking. It's really not all that bad!

CHAPTER 33

LOOK AROUND YOU

One discipline I've cherished through the years is my quiet time with the Lord. As a routine in the morning, I get my coffee, and hang out with God for a while, just me, my coffee, my bible and my prayer journal. It's been in these quiet times that God has done His greatest work in my life. I've been prompted, reminded, scolded, loved, encouraged, and guided by His word. He is faithful! I've come to never second guess God.

Never doubt where God plants you. I look back on the neighbors we've had through the years and how our lives have intertwined. When we lived in our second home, the boys were preschool age. At the end of the street lived Joyce, a stay at home mom with two kids. Joyce became the best babysitter we could have ever hoped for. Our boys learned how to swim in her pool at a young age. I never recall a day when I worried about them, but maybe I should have.

Joyce has a daughter, Jana, that was the same age as our son Benji, his endearing name then, that we are told never to use again. It was very common for the two of them to play together. In December of 2001, Jana and Benji were five years old. Right before the children's Christmas program at church, they decided to play hair stylist. Benji said, "It was Jana's idea." Yupper! When Benji came home from playing,

his bangs had been hacked so much that all you could see was a jagged line almost to the crown of his head.
Now Benji had beautiful red hair so you could pick him out in a crowd, something I found to be helpful at times. There was no hiding his haircut in the Christmas program. Fortunately his hair grew fast and it became another funny story to share. We felt blessed to have great neighbors, especially Joyce.

Becky was another wonderful baby sitter. She watched several kids of different ages. One day while in Becky's care, the kids piled into the car to go to preschool. Jason, was sitting in the passenger seat. This was prior to the mandatory seatbelt laws. Unfortunately, the car door wasn't completely latched. As the driver took off, the car door flew open and Jason tumbled out of the car. Once she realized this little kid, my son, was lying on the pavement, she stopped the car. I'm sure she went into panic mode. I know I would have! Fortunately, he got up and got back in the car with only a few scapes. Thank you Jesus! Sadly, Becky passed away last year, and her son John, asked Jason to do the funeral. How special is that?

When we moved to our third home, George and Betty lived across the street from us. They were a quiet couple that stayed to themselves. When George was diagnosed with cancer, I felt prompted to go and talk to him. George and Betty were about the same age as my parents. As I sat with George in his living room we talked about his health and his heart. That day he allowed me to pray with him. George had tears in his eyes. Times like this aren't easy, as you never know how the person will respond. However, when

God is the prompter of an idea, you can count on Him to go before you and prepare the way.

Psalm 37:23-24: "The Lord directs the steps of the godly. He delights in every detail of their lives. Though they stumble, they will not fall, for the Lord holds them by the hand."

After a few years, the lovely family that lived next door to us moved out and a couple from out of town moved in. It's rare to meet someone for the first time and know that person is someone you're going to like, but that's how it was this time. My new neighbor was similar in age to me and we had a lot of the same interests. She had a contagious laughter and, above all, she loved the Lord. We soon became good friends. Her husband was an executive at a local business, and was always well dressed. He was much quieter than his wife, to the point that he seemed aloof and distracted in his thoughts. In conversations, it frequently felt like his mind was somewhere else.

One day, while my friend and I were taking a walk she shared with me that her husband wasn't acting himself. She described a few of his behaviors that raised a red flag for me. He would often travel for work and would be gone over the weekends. I had worked at Bayer HealthCare for many years and knew that most business travel was done during the week so people could be home on the weekends with their families. I said to my friend, "Do you think he's having an affair?" She said confidently, "No!" I wasn't convinced.

One evening, several months after our conversation, I came home from getting groceries and Duane said, "You need to go next door right away." We had been notified that our neighbor's husband had a massive heart attack while he was out of town. The hospital didn't want his wife to be alone. I rushed next door to find my neighbor curled up on the floor crying uncontrollably. I nestled next to her with disbelief that this was happening. Once she got control of her emotions, she was able to tell me more than I ever hoped to know. Her husband had died of a massive heart attack while with another woman. The pain and the grief of his loss and deception were unbearable!

For the next several days we tried to sort things out, like who needed to be contacted and many more difficult decisions. It was painful and tragic! When you're grieving to this degree you can't think clearly. There are no words to express the sadness and heartbreak that I saw in my friend.

This tragedy has many lessons for us.

1. God can never be deceived. We can fool people, but we can't fool Him.
2. It's also a reminder of how much our choices affect others.
3. Lastly, there's redemption for those who seek it.

The day they moved in, God knew that my neighbor and I would share this part of her journey. I wish it never happened, but it did, and I will always be humbled that God chose me to be her neighbor and friend at such a devastating time in her life. She has since moved on and remarried, and is living a happy life. God healed her broken heart. We all need people we can trust and rely on. There's a reason and purpose for where we are, let's not miss it!

CHAPTER 34

IT'S EASY TO GIVE UP, BUT DON'T

In 2003, we built our dream house. We have lived in four homes, all within a fifteen mile radius of each other. I guess we like the area. About a year after we built, an older couple built right next door. Ron was a salesman and very outgoing. Phyllis was quiet and stayed to herself. It took years for me to get to know Phyllis. Her self esteem seemed to revolve around her more confident husband. Even when she gave him a hard time it seemed to be a cover for the softness she was hesitant to reveal. She wanted to appear tough, but she wasn't. Suspicious, she was.

For example, a young mom in the neighborhood wanted to invite several of us ladies out for dinner together as a way to get to know each other. But, instead of mailing the invitations, she put a note in each of our mailboxes. When Phyllis got her invitation, she was furious to think someone had opened her mailbox. She returned the note to the young mom, telling her to never do that again. Over the years we watched Phyllis mellow. We would talk more often and she began to take a liking to me. She would even initiate conversation and she and Ron began buying us the nicest of Christmas gifts! Phyllis and I became good friends! The walls were down and she could trust me.

Ron had every tool and gadget a guy would want. He helped Duane do small projects around our house. He was our go-to-guy for fixing things. Ron would get up before the dew was dry on the grass and be outside working on his lawn. He was a perfectionist! They had the most beautiful flowers. No matter how hard I tried, my flowers never looked as good as theirs.

Ron loved his Harley Davidson Motorcycle. In 2014 he fell at work and injured his hand. It was bothering him so much that he couldn't ride his Harley. His doctor told him he could repair his hand through surgery, so he could ride again. In late February 2015, Ron went in for hand surgery which was to be a simple procedure. Everything seemed to go well and they released him to go home. As Phyllis was driving him home, she looked over at Ron to find him slumped in his seat and unconscious. She drove to a nearby fire station and alerted the paramedics. They were unable to revive him, so they rushed him to the hospital. Ron never regained consciousness. He stayed on life support for several days before passing. To my knowledge they never found out the cause of death.

I was with Mike, their only son, and Phyllis when Ron took his last breath. We all knew it was just a matter of time. Phyllis asked me to help her find something to wear to the funeral. It was a privilege. We shopped until we found the right outfit. We spent many hours together after his passing. Our friendship grew stronger and more meaningful as Phyllis began to open up to me. We talked about God and her relationship with Him. When she told me she wasn't sure about going to heaven and said, "I hope I'm ready." I said Phyllis, "You don't have to wonder, you can be sure!" She prayed that day to accept Christ as her personal Savior.

From then on, we would often joke about being neighbors in heaven.

A couple years after Ron passed, Phyllis was driving to a doctor's appointment, a place she had been many times before. But on this day, she got lost and confused and pulled off to the side of the road because she didn't know where she was at. She slowly regained her senses but, by the time she got to her doctor's appointment she was so upset by her confusion that the doctor immediately called her son, Mike, and had him come to get her. She was later diagnosed with Dementia and could no longer drive. She would ask me to take her to appointments so Mike didn't have to take time off work. Phyllis became the kind of neighbor that I could walk next door with my cup of coffee and we would sit and talk about everything. She told me numerous times that I was her best friend. We had come along way as neighbors. She had become an equally good friend to me.

Once she got to the point where she could no longer take care of herself, we went looking for an assisted living place. After visiting many places, I believe God directed us to The Elkhart Place. We were impressed by the staff and the activities they had planned for their residence. It's been a good home for Phyllis. Her memory continues to decline. A few months ago, during my visit, she didn't recognize me. It brought tears to my eyes. Dementia is a sad disease. It's very hard to watch someone you care about forget how to do simple things. It breaks my heart!

GOD'S PERFECT STRATEGY

As we look back at the relationships God has put in our paths, I am reminded of Deuteronomy 31:8, "The LORD himself goes before you and will be with you; he will never leave you or forsake you. Do not be afraid; do not be discouraged."

God may not call you to help with the intimate details of a neighbor's declining health, but wherever you are, there's a reason for it! We must not overlook the moment we're living in. As we open our eyes to the people around us, there's one calling we all share, to be available and accessible. There is a reason those people are in our world. I believe the more we're wrapped up in ourselves the less we notice the needs of others. God please forgive me for all the times I've missed an opportunity to serve someone else.

Many people need to know God's perfect strategy for their life. They may be totally lost and need someone to redirect their path. Let's not miss the opportunity!

CHAPTER 35

ROBBED OF JOY

In the winter of 2003 my world went quiet. No energy, loss of interest, isolation, and fear swept over me. I curled up in a ball in my favorite chair and slept. If I left the house, Duane would go with me. In the store, I would hide behind him to not see or be seen. I can't explain it!

As months passed, a friend reached out to me. She offered to come over and sit with me. I knew I could trust her. She prayed with me, read scripture, and she never judged me! It took months to get through it.

The Bible refers to people who are brokenhearted, downcast, troubled, miserable and full of despair. In the book of Psalms, David writes about his anguish, loneliness and guilt from sin.

"Why are you downcast, O my soul? Why so disturbed within me? Put your hope in God for I will yet praise him, my Savior and my God." Ps 42:11

Elijah was discouraged, weary and afraid. Jonah was angry and wanted to run away. Job suffered great loss, devastation, and physical illness.

Although I didn't experience many of the feelings, expressed in scripture, I felt empty and lost. What had changed within me?

When I finally pulled through I was different. Prior to my depression, I had little sympathy for this disease. With little knowledge it seemed to me people just needed to get a grip. They needed to get over it and move on. Quit complaining, and feeling sorry for yourself. No more sad faces!

Today I have great empathy! My heart grieves for those who struggle with depression. It's real and it hurts!

God never left me! He heard my silence. He felt my pain. He understood me. He never stopped loving me! He used this rocky part of my journey to educate me. He is our best teacher!

I thank my friend Brenda for sitting with me, and my husband Duane for waiting patiently without judgement. If you are going through depression, remember this verse in Deuteronomy 31: 8. "Do not be afraid or discouraged, for the Lord will personally go ahead of you. He will be with you; he will neither fail you nor abandon you." I use this verse a lot.

CHAPTER 36

WHEN WE LEAST EXPECT IT

In 2018 Duane and I met our 41 year old son, Ben, in Banff, Alberta Canada. Banff was a place we all had on our bucket list. Duane and I have been to many places in our travels, but for me, Banff was the most beautiful of all. It is known for its turquoise, glacier-fed lakes. It's located in the Canadian Rockies. We rented a condo in Canmore, just outside of Banff. If you ever get to Banff, you must visit Lake Louise, it will take your breath away! Ben loves photography, and is very good at it. If you know anything about photography you know that the best time to shoot is early morning or at dusk. So the three of us got up at the crack of dawn to go photo shooting. Big yawn! We not only got to see our son do something he loves, but we learned to appreciate the patience it takes to get the best picture.

As we were sitting around in the condo one evening, Ben asked his dad, "If you could have anything you want for Christmas, what would it be?" After thinking about it, Duane said, "For you to have a wife!" Ben smiled, getting the answer he expected. Little did we know that Ben was going to introduce us to someone very special on this trip. He told us, "I'm coming home for Christmas and I'm bringing someone with me." Huge smile! Cartwheels! YIPPEE!

Ben doesn't just bring anyone home, so we knew this was promising! The even bigger surprise was that Jillian Pade, his girlfriend, lived in Sydney, Australia. As I mentioned before, we've always given our sons freedom to go and do what they want, but Australia? Duane and I never wanted to be an obstacle or reason for them not to go or pursue what they wanted to, but this was on the other side of the world. WOW! We had to let that one soak in.

Ben arranged for us to FaceTime Jillian and her parents, Peter and Valerie Pade. Thank goodness for technology! We were all a bit nervous hoping it would go smoothly and that we wouldn't say anything stupid. Usually introductions like this consist of small talk and sizing each other up through this real time camera called FaceTime. So we all scrunched together on the couch because the camera was only so big. We made sure there wasn't any food in our teeth and that our hair was combed, you know the drill.

The first thing I noticed was Jillian's beautiful smile and her Aussie accent. Her mom and dad looked normal, so that was a good start. They were a lovely couple and easy to talk to. Valerie and I did most of the talking. Women can usually find something to say. Our first impression of this family was remarkable. There was something very comforting about meeting them. We finished our lovely trip in Banff and headed home. It was always hard saying goodbye to Ben because we were never sure when we'd see him again. This time was different since he was coming home for Christmas and that was only a few months away. We came home from Canada feeling a sense of hope that, perhaps, maybe this time, our son had met his future wife.
As we prepared for Ben and Jill's visit for Christmas we decided to stay with our normal family traditions.

After I retired in 2017, we began a new gift giving tradition. All the years I had worked we would have several hundred dollars saved in a separate account just for Christmas. This resource was no longer going to be there, so we thought it would be wise to adjust right away. We had been wise by staying out of debt and building a nest egg in investments, but we still wanted to be responsible.

Our new Christmas gift giving tradition was based on the number of recorded gifts that Jesus received from the Three Wise Men, gold, frankincense and myrrh. According to the gospel He got three gifts. In years past, our Christmas tree was packed with so many gifts it covered every inch around the Christmas tree and then some. If three gifts were enough for Jesus, then three gifts are enough for us. Since it was my idea for the three gifts, I could also make the rules; so just because you got three boxes to open, didn't necessarily mean there was only one item in each box. Let's just say, I broke my own rule and I took some heat for it. We've always loved celebrating Christmas, and giving gifts, so I'm slowly adjusting to this new three gift giving idea. UGH!

My dilemma became what to buy for Jillian. We knew nothing about what she liked or her taste. Deep down inside, I didn't want to get too personal. I wanted to protect my heart. Ben had been in relationships before and when they didn't work out it was disappointing and sad. As he got older, in his upper thirties, we wondered if he would ever get married. I remember telling him, Ben if you don't get married, please find out what God wants you to do in your life, because your life has a purpose. It's one thing to be single, it's another not to have a fulfilling purpose.

We bought Jillian a Starfish Project bracelet that was too big for her small wrist. Starfish Project Ministry is in China and was started by a girl in our hometown. It's an amazing ministry and the bracelet would have a significant meaning. We would later learn that Jillian doesn't wear much jewelry at all. Lessons learned. She received three gifts to open just like everyone else. She was so generous in her giving to our family. Her gifts from Australia were so thoughtful. Her parents even sent gifts. What a sweet surprise!

We learned a lot about Jillian that week over Christmas. From the get-go, we knew she would be a lot of fun! On our ride home from the airport she broke out in song singing the Notre Dame fight song! She knew every word and stayed on tune. It was like whoa, who does this?! She knew we were big Notre Dame fans so she took the time to memorize the song and lyrics, I mean, you go girl! We were impressed!

We learned about her strengths and patience. She and Ben both remained single waiting on the right one. Jill is a strong woman and very comfortable with herself. She made herself at home and became a part of us right from the beginning. We would learn about her work as an Interior Designer. She owns Pade by Design in Sydney, AUS.
She and Ben have the same interests and would be a wonderful support for each other. Above all, they both love Jesus. Our prayers had been answered!

They got engaged in 2019 and were married in Australia November 7, 2019. Duane and I were fortunate to be able to attend the wedding in Sydney. Her parents were gracious enough to let us stay with them for three weeks. That's a long time to open your home up to someone you've never met before. They were so gracious! With the cost of traveling and the wedding, this gesture on their part helped us a lot. We will always remember their hospitality and kindness to us.

Ben and Jill put a lot of thought into the wedding as most couples do. The church they chose was small and intimate. The reception was out of this world! Everything about it was picture perfect! We were so happy for them. They had waited so long for this special day.

During our time at the Pade's home, Valerie and I had many good talks. She told me about a time she was praying for Jill and she heard God say in her spirit to "pray for the man". Pray for the man? That man is my son! Once they were married, we accepted our new reality, that our youngest son would be living overseas. Ultimately, as a parent, we wanted our children to find their own place in life. If this was a part of God's plan, then we were all in.

Sometimes we lose trust and wonder if God is going to answer our request. We know He can! We believe and know He is all powerful, all knowing and all present! We know what we know, but when we don't see anything happening we begin to doubt. Just because we can't see what's happening doesn't mean God isn't working. When Ben told me how he and Jillian met, I knew it was God all along. They connected on a dating sight, 10,000 miles apart. Their relationship started and grew through FaceTime. Because of their age and place in life, they didn't waste anytime getting to what was important to them. From the day they were born, just a year apart, God knew they would someday marry. Just like when Kathy and I walked to kindergarten together, God knew our kids would be married one day. When we walk with the Lord, he is absolutely the best tour guide!

Thanking God for His perfect strategy!

Ben and Jillian's wedding
reception in Sydney, AU
was absolutely magical!

CHAPTER 37

DON'T LOSE HEART

What is it about God we don't get? Why do we doubt his timing? Why do we question if he hears us? Why do we chase our purpose separate from his? He is the only one who is 100% faithful! He created us, shaped us, prepared us, and patiently waits for us to get to the point where He can trust us with His plan. It's not God that is slow, it's us! I love the symbolic example in the Bible about the Potter and the clay. God created each of us to have a relationship with Him. This is so important to remember. He created us so that we would know Him. We have children so we can have a relationship with them.

These next few verses are astounding to me! The Bible is so precise about our creation. Listen closely to these words.

Psalm 139:13-16 says, "You made all the delicate, inner parts of my body and knit them together in my mother's womb. Thank you for making me so wonderfully complex! Your workmanship is marvelous, how well I know it. You watched me as I was being formed in utter seclusion, as I was woven together in the dark of the womb. You saw me before I was born. Every day of my life was recorded in your book. Every moment was laid out before a single day had passed." Wow, Wow and Wow!

In Exodus 4:11-12, God says to Moses, "Who makes a person's mouth? Who decides whether people speak or do not speak, hear or do not hear, see or do not see? It is I, the Lord. Now go! I will be with you as you speak, and I will instruct you in what to say."

If you want to read the rest of the story about Moses, he was reluctant to obey God and God got angry with him. God is gracious and merciful, but if we miss what He has for us, we're the only ones to blame.

My second cousin just finished serving six years in prison. It's her story to tell so I won't go into the details. While she was incarcerated we wrote faithfully, and studied portions of the Bible together. Her letters were honest, but always positive. I'm stilled amazed at how well she has handled it.

She was baptized in a large water tank while in prison and attended Bible studies and helped many other women. Her mom, my cousin, has a BIG heart! Whenever my cousin would send a gift box to her daughter she would fill it to the brim so it could be shared with other cell mates. They realized that many of the women incarcerated don't have the same resources or support. That's what I call kindness and generosity. Perhaps those gestures of kindness can help someone in prison not lose heart.

In 2012, Duane walked into work, like any other normal day. But this day would be anything but normal. He wasn't at work long until he was told to go up to the front office.
At that point they told him, that after 38 years, the company was cutting back and they no longer needed him. He was out of a job. They had the audacity to let him go just one

year before retirement. It was a crushing blow! I had never seen my husband like this before. His job loss lead him into depression. We made financial adjustments and did what needed to be done. As time went on, it became another example of God's faithfulness. When bad things happen, our days can look dark and gloomy. It's a lot like a dreary and cloudy day. We know the sun is still shining, high above the clouds, even when we can't see it.

What I learned in the days to come is just how suppressed that job of 38 years had made my husband. He went from a confined factory job to a part time job selling cars. He was now working with the public and he loved it! After getting out of the factory he became a changed man. Instead of standing at a machine all day, he was interacting with people. It was the best thing that could've happened to him. I'm so proud of him for trying something new!

CHAPTER 38

JUST DO IT!

The slogan "Just Do It", doesn't allow for excuses, just get the job done! Stop looking for reasons not to do something. Ouch! That spoke to me. We've all been there and done that. We make convenient excuses for ourselves. I've come to realize I have fewer regrets over the things I've done than the things I haven't done.

One evening back in the 1980s, I attended a Women's Ministry meeting that would change my life. The speaker was a nurse, and her topic was geared toward outreach. She shared about the work that was being done by Child Protective Services (CPS) and the need they had for volunteers. A volunteer for CPS would be trained by professionals and then paired with a case worker to spend time with a family that had been found to be abusive to their children. On my way home that night, I felt a strong call by God to get involved. How did I know it was God? I believe when God moves us to see beyond ourselves and to acknowledge the gifts He has given us, He opens our eyes to those places where He wants us to serve. I knew that I knew that I knew I needed to do this!

The CPS training required me to be gone a few hours a week during the evening. Once you're assigned to a family, CPS requires you to meet with that family at least once a week, preferably twice a week. It was going to be a big commitment. Our own boys were only in grade school at the time. I could never have done this without Duane's help and support.

After going through the training, they assigned me to a case worker who had been dealing with a family in a nearby town. I met the case worker and she took me to the apartment where I would meet the mom and her two young daughters. The case worker went with me the first time, then I was on my own. CPS had far more cases than case workers so as soon as a volunteer was trained they were given a family. The night the case worker and I met to go to the home, she informed me of the situation on our drive over. I honestly don't remember all the details she shared and maybe it's just as well. We would be meeting the mother, Ann, and her two little girls. The father worked evenings, so he wouldn't be at home when we got there. I was glad!

When we got to the area, we drove down a dark alley alongside a green two story apartment house. We parked in the back alley and walked a short distance, that at times felt like forever, to a narrow and steep staircase that led to the second story apartment. The stairs were old and the old neighborhood felt very unsafe. I have very little recollection of our first meeting, but I will never forget my next one. At the conclusion of my first visit, the case worker had me set up a time with Ann for the following week when I would come back. Ann didn't have a phone, so if anything changed, there was no easy way she could contact me.

The following week, I parked in front of the house instead of the back alley. I walked to the back and up that long narrow staircase. It was the only entry to her apartment. It was the time of year when the days were shorter, so it was dark when I arrived. I frequently talked to God asking him to protect me, because honestly, I was scared and wondered what I would encounter. I knew in my heart that God called me to do this, so it seemed reasonable to me that He would protect me.

I knocked on the door and Ann asked me to come in. I could tell she wasn't crazy about my being there. She wanted to know what I was going to do, etc., etc., and why I had been assigned to her and her family. I'm not sure what I said, but she must have been okay with it. I had to assure her many times that I was there to help her and the girls. The apartment was unkept and down right dirty. Her two little girls were preschool age. Becky was the oldest and Linda the youngest. I had arrived after dinner, so the girls would be going to bed shortly. Ann and I talked for a while just getting acquainted. I had to build her trust if this was going to work.

After a while I said to her, why don't you just sit here and relax and I'll clean up the kitchen. It's something us neat freaks say when we want to do it ourselves. She smiled and said, "Okay." As I walked back into the kitchen there were pots and pans sitting on the stove, so I thought I'd begin doing dishes. The apartment was very small, so I could be in the kitchen and still see and talk to Ann while she was sitting in the living room. You might wonder why I would start with home maintenance when this family is accused of abusing their daughters. First of all, it was my comfort level and I had to start somewhere. Also, there are many reasons for abuse. For this couple, it was anger, confinement and ignorance.

#1 Anger - from feeling trapped, broke and isolated

Ann's husband was an alcoholic who spent his paychecks at the bar

Ann had no car

Ann had no money

They had no air-conditioning in those hot steaming summer days

#2 Confinement - a feeling of being imprisoned in your own home

#3 Ignorance - they didn't know how to deal with conflict and had no friends or resources to help them.

As I removed the lid off the pan on the stove, my eyes must have gotten as big as saucers! There were hundreds of tiny maggots thriving in the bottom of the pot on top of boiled potatoes. Who knew how long they had been in there. I let out a big sigh. I hoped she didn't hear. I asked her if she had a trash bag. She better have a trash bag! Thankfully, she did. Once I got the kitchen cleaned, I asked Ann if she'd like me to help get the girls ready for bed. Both girls needed a bath, but I didn't want to be too assertive as it wasn't my place. At that point, Ann smiled at me, and I could tell she wasn't used to anyone lending a hand. My hope was to model a godly woman and mother so that she could see there's another way of parenting. Modeling is a powerful tool to use especially when it comes to protecting children.

I continued to go to Ann's place twice a week. Our relationship grew as she began to trust me. Trust is the glue that holds a relationship together. Ann had to realize I wasn't there to take her children away from her. I was there to help her become a better her. When you help the parent, you help the child. It was amazing to me to watch how Ann's whole demeanor changed once she started to feel better about herself. She shared many things with me. I encouraged her to do her hair and wear some makeup to help her self esteem and her relationship with Ed. I showed her how to clean her house so it would be a safer and cleaner place for them. You could easily see the kind of life the girls had. Their teeth were rotting from eating so much candy. I'm sure at times candy was a meal for them. Linda had uncontrolled temper tantrums where she would sit on the floor and bang her head against the wall as hard as she could. Becky was a couple years older and she liked me a lot. Even though Becky was little, I could see a different kind of curiosity in her. She seemed to notice something different about me and I could tell.

With Ann's permission, Becky was allowed to come home with me for a couple hours. She stood on a kitchen chair next to me at the sink and helped me fix potato salad. We washed dishes together and just hung out. Becky was the sweeter of the two girls. Linda was a pistol. I often had concern about how much of the right foods they were actually getting to eat. There was a family restaurant in town that wasn't too far from their apartment, so we went there on several occasions. I'd tell them they could order whatever they wanted. Going to a restaurant was a treat for all of us.

Ann's husband was always out of the picture. He worked nights and would stop at the bar on his way home. I only recall meeting him one time. He was polite and quiet. He didn't seem like the mean or angry kind. Ann was the one who had been reported as abusing the girls. Every now and then, I could see her anger flare up and she would jokingly threaten them in my presence. She knew she wouldn't dare hurt them in anyway in front of me. She could trust me, but I was there to ultimately protect those girls.

During the time I knew them, they lived in at least three different places. When I visited Ann and the girls at one of their homes, I could hear mice gnawing on the couch as I sat on it. The girls would laugh and laugh. They thought it was hysterical! They had no fear of mice. I sat as close to the edge as I could ready to make a mad dash out the door should one of those little critters peak his pesky head out at me. It was creepy!

There were two unforgettable moments for me with this family. One of them was when Ann went to a pay phone one evening to call me. When I picked up the phone she said, "Karen, I CLEANED the house. Can you come over?" As I walked into her spotless home, I felt tears welling up in my eyes to think how far she had come from those maggots crawling in the pot on the stove. She had learned how to take pride in herself and had changed as a mother before my very eyes.

The other time was during a visit with Ann when she asked me if I would go and do the same thing for her friend Brenda as I had done for her. Brenda lived in the downstairs apartment and Ann upstairs, so they got to know each other pretty well. I told Ann I was willing to go see her. As we walked down to Brenda's, I wasn't sure what I was getting myself into. Brenda was from the deep south and had gotten married at a very young age.

She had five children, four girls and one boy. As I began to sit down on the couch, her children swarmed me, like they'd never seen another human being before. They wanted to touch me, comb my hair and sit on my lap. These children, lovely children, were craving affection and attention. The youngest of her five children was a little boy. You could look at him and see an armor of protection. For a little kid, he was guarded and very husky. He sat in front of their TV, and if he would even look like he was going to change the channel, his mom, Brenda would raise a large switch like a branch off a tree and threaten to hit him with it. Brenda was a tough cookie. I'm not sure what she thought of me, but I felt out of my league.

There were times I would go home and cry my eyes out. I was over my head and this was just a taste of what so many children experience on a daily basis. After a few years of helping Ann, I felt like I had done all I could. They eventually relocated to Southern Indiana and we lost touch. I never worked with Brenda. I notified CPS of their circumstances out of concern for the children. I'm not sure if they ever followed up or not. I wish I could have done more, but my first priority was to my own family. I felt I had given all I could in time, modeling, energy and love to Ann, Linda and Becky. It was an experience that changed my life. It changed how I view the abuser. I had to ask myself, "What would I be like under the same circumstances?" We all want to believe we are above hurting our children and most of us are. But after seeing first hand the lifestyle and lack of resources and the feeling of being trapped, it gave me a greater understanding of how easily tempers can flare and abuse can happen. It's tragic and children deserve better. Parents need help and love also! They need to know someone is on their side when they need an escape.

CHAPTER 39

BRAGGING RIGHTS

My husband loves football! He played all four years in high school. In his senior year, 1970, the team won the state title. He loves having sons that share his passion for the game. In 2006, Duane started volunteering as an usher for the Notre Dame football games. Over the past few years he has been a field usher, giving him a front row seat to the game. Notre Dame is just a short 20 miles from our house. It is ranked #19 in National Universities, and one of the best Catholic Colleges in America.

The campus of Notre Dame is like no other. In the fall, as the trees turn reddish orange and yellow, the Golden Dome is a spectacular backdrop for any photographer. So, to be able to walk along the sidelines of the Irish football field and be paid for it is any football sports enthusiast's dream come true. Not only is it about the game, but about the many fans and celebrities who travel long distance, or pick up a quick ticket while in the area. Duane has met stars live Owen Wilson, Vince Vaughn, Regis Philbin, Lou Holtz, Condoleeza Rice and many more. He met Garth Brooks while ushering at his concert in the football stadium. Every year he looks forward to seeing ushers, like himself, who return year after year to enjoy the games.

When we first got married we knew so little about each other. We were kids! The one thing that I mentioned early on, is

how his maturity attracted me. After dating a bunch of knuckleheads I knew what I was looking for.
He has attributes of being a hard worker, organized, thorough, detail oriented, prompt, dependable, consistent, thoughtful, helpful with a "getter done" mentality. If a light bulb burns out or a battery dies... he's on it. There's also another side of Duane that could be interpreted as his soft side. He loves ambience! Put on music, dim the lights, light the candles. He's romantic! We feel our home is calming, relaxing and comfortable because of the atmosphere. It was that way until we got Murphy. Murphy is our 65 pound Mini Golden Doodle, that is neither mini nor golden. He is black and white and big, but we love our Murphy!

After Duane retired in 2015 he set up a workshop in our basement. I call it Duane's Hobby Shop. Since retirement, he has handcrafted wood carvings, made candles, soap, bookends, clocks, tables, and much more. He is a craftsman and he enjoys giving his creations to those who appreciate them. The Christmas of 2020, we prepared 12 gift bags filled with handmade items and delivered them to neighbors, family and friends. When we stopped at someone's home and handed them a homemade gift, we hoped it would be a blessing to them. Need I say more? I am so proud of my husband!

CHAPTER 40

JUST YOU AND ME BABE

Our nest has been empty for many years now. We're back where we started, but much older now. We are both loving retirement! We stay up late and sleep as long as we want. When we wake up and get our coffee, we sit together and solve all the world's problems. Overall we're not doing so well in that area. We always find something to talk about. Even if we don't have much to say, just being together and hanging out in our relaxing home, and not having to rush off to work makes it a great day!

I love my husband more than anyone on the face of the earth! We've been through so much as we've navigated the last 50 years. We started out broke and naive. We moved to Colorado and back to Indiana. As you'll recall from prior pages, we lost his dad in a car accident six weeks after we were married. We built three homes and raised two amazing sons. They are amazing because of God, not us. We both lost jobs. We fought and we recovered. We were strapped financially at times. We worried and wondered. Duane's nickname for me is Wonder Woman because I'm always wondering about something.

Duane and I have learned to laugh more and not take ourselves or each other so seriously. We've come to pause more before reacting and to listen better and wait patiently. We're trying! Every day we pray together, at least at meal times. We are always thankful!

When you climb mountains together, and venture down rocky cliffs without falling apart or letting go, that's pretty special! Fifty years is a long time to be married, and sadly in our culture few make it. Endurance builds character, and character makes us who we are.

We all have vulnerable times in our lives. Where the rubber meets the road we have to make a decision. Many years ago, I was restless in my marriage. I went to the only source I knew that cared more about Duane and I than anyone else. I got on my knees and prayed, and you can better believe God answered my prayer. He healed my heart.

God has allowed me to share my story with other women who were on the brink of divorce, by choice. The one is still married. The other left her husband for many years, only to find that grass had a fungus too. She is now back with her husband, who remained faithful through it all.

Our stories are never wasted if we're willing to risk our pride. It's easy to lose our self when we try to live up to someone else's expectations. We're all flawed! We all have wrinkles in our underwear. Let's run the race set before us. Let's stay in our lane. Let's all agree to go to the Prince of Peace for counseling. He knows His stuff! I like to say Jesus was a carpenter; He can fix things.

CHAPTER 41

A REASON FOR EVERYTHING

January 2022, our lives were shaken. Just months before, in November of 2021, Rachael, our daughter-in-law, was experiencing mild discomfort and thought she should be checked out by her doctor. The exam showed she had a 9 cm cyst on one of her ovaries. The results of a CT scan revealed the return of her breast cancer (from several years ago) in the form of metastasized lesions in a number of areas throughout her body. After surgery to remove her ovaries, she started chemotherapy and radiation.

Jason and Rachael have experienced God's grace and mercy. Rachael believes God put an angel, David, in her path at Cleveland Clinic. He was an elderly man sitting in the same waiting room. After some small talk he asked Rachael why she was there. With tears she told him her story. He stood up and asked, "Can I pray for you?". She said, "Absolutely!" She shared with him how she believes in the power of prayer, and that she would value his prayers. Rachael explained to us how he prayed for healing in the name of Jesus. It was a powerful moment right there in the waiting room. She told him how she and Jason were looking through the eyes of faith and not fear. She said, he looked at her straight in the eyes and said, "Don't let worry take over. That is completely from the devil!" I praise God for David's faithfulness, and courage to reach out to Rachael in such a meaningful way. Jason and Rachael have great faith!

To say the least, January was emotionally painful for Duane and I, as we tried to wrap our arms and hearts around this unexpected news. I believe it's been the power of prayer from so many people, and their positive determination to not give Satan a foothold in their lives that has made us all a lot stronger.

In December, two weeks before Ben and Jill came home for Christmas, I began having knee pain like I'd never experienced before. It was difficult to stand for any length of time. As time went on, the pain extended from my lower back down the outside of my leg. It was excruciating pain, and I don't use that word lightly. When you can't sit, sleep, lie down or stand without pain, it controls your body, mind, and emotions. The pain in my leg was riveting. I was prescribed Oxycodone, and that didn't help. After two MRI's they found a torn meniscus in my knee and a herniated disc and pinched nerve in my back. I had surgery to fix the knee and an epidural for the back pain. It's been several months since my surgery and I am doing much better.

There's a reason for everything. Why this? Why now? Since God causes all things to work together for good, we have a right to ask God why. I believe He wants us to know exactly what He's up to, in His time. When I was in so much pain, I listened to a lot of messages by Rick Warren, and Charles Stanley. With pain, I found it easier to listen than to read. Wouldn't you know it, every message hit home. Charles Stanley's sermon on "God's Purpose in the Storm", was my favorite. He says, "God will send a storm into your life to get your attention. Some people only need a strong wind, other people need a hurricane".

GOD'S PERFECT STRATEGY

On January 28, 2022, Duane and I celebrated our 50th wedding anniversary in a clinic for my MRI. We had to chuckle. We'll celebrate this summer with our family. The day we were married, God knew it all. He knew every challenge we would face, every highlight, every memory, every birth, every death. It's comforting to know He knows our future. We trust Him now and forever, because He has the perfect strategy!

CHAPTER 42

IT IS WELL WITH MY SOUL

I want to share this quote from Helen Keller one more time. As I carefully process her words, it brings hope for each trial and adversity we face.

"Character cannot be developed in ease and quiet. Only through experience of trial and suffering can the soul be strengthened, vision cleared, ambition inspired, and success achieved." (Helen Keller n.d.)

Duane and I are looking forward to the next chapter in our marriage. We know there will be times of blessing, trials, challenges, and testing. We decided a long time ago that His plan is so much better than anything we could ever dream up.

In this memoir, I haven't shared about all the pot holes we've hit and detours we've made in life. Instead, I'll follow the advice of a former boss who said, "If there's no value added, don't do it." My prayer through this project, is that my words and stories will reflect threads of hope for all of us. No journey is perfect on this earth. The best outcome is when we learn and grow from our trials. When we allow them to shape us into better people.

Several years ago, I came across scripture that really spoke to me. It has become my life verse.

Philippians 1:9-11, reflects my hearts desire. I've worded it, as *my* prayer to God.

Dear Lord,
"And this is my prayer, that my love may abound more and more in knowledge and depth of insight, so that I may be able to discern what is best and may be pure and blameless until the day of Christ, filled with the fruit of righteousness that comes through Jesus Christ to the glory and praise of God."

My prayer for my family is that we will represent God well. That we will have a calming effect on others, excluding US football and basketball games and rugby and soccer in Australia. I hope I've covered all the exceptions. Big smile!

Jason and Ben, we will forever be your mom and dad. We will love and care about you for the rest of our lives. Although your paths have been very different, you have both made the best and ultimate decision to follow Jesus! We are beyond grateful!

Rachael and Jillian, we love you like our own. God could not have given me, the mother of sons, two better daughter-in-laws. I pray we live out the verse from Psalms, "Be still and know that I am God." Walk by faith and not by sight. Let's do our best.

Haley and Natalie, you are giving us memories to cherish. We love your smiles and hugs! We love spending time with you! My prayer for you is found in Matthew 6:33, "Seek first the kingdom of God and His righteousness, and all the other things will be added unto you." When you find yourself in a difficult spot in life, always remember that God is with you. My prayer is that you will spot evil and flee from it! Run as far away from sin as possible. You will never regret it!

To my dear husband, thank you for loving me well. Thank you for your faithfulness and your unending love for our family. Thank you for being a man that I can be proud of! Thank you for giving me a life full of fun and adventure. Thank you for never giving up on us!

To my mom and dad, thank you for choosing Jesus!

Someday, when I stand before my heavenly Father, nothing in the world will matter, but what He thinks of me and who He says I am. He is my Father! I am His daughter, and He knows my name! When we die, the only thing that will matter is our relationship with Jesus. Let's make it our earthly priority to know Him.

Lord, someday, in Your time, Gods Perfect Strategy will direct me to my eternal home. I will be going to the house you have prepared for me. My heart rejoices just thinking about it! While I wait, use me to reflect your love and kindness to those in my corner of the world.

John 14:1-4 NIV "Do not let your hearts be troubled. Trust in God, trust also in me. In my Father's house are many rooms, if it were not so, I would have told you. And if I go to prepare a place for you, I will come back and take you to be with me that you also may be where I am. You know the way to the place I am going." Amen! Amen!

ABOUT THE AUTHOR

"The greatest thing I can say about my mom is that she's the real deal. She's a woman of deep faith who deserves a great deal of credit for the man I am today. As a child, I vividly remember seeing her at the kitchen table each morning reading her Bible, praying and journaling before heading off to work. That intimate relationship with Christ has not wavered over all these years. In addition to her faith, I've always admired her courage and can-do attitude. While she never attended college, she refused to allow that to stop her from succeeding in the corporate world. In 2017, she retired after 33 years from Bayer HealthCare. Her life has been spent poured out in service to others. I have no doubt that this book will encourage and challenge you in your faith."

Jason R. Thompson
Oldest son of Karen (Balyeat) Thompson

REFERENCES

Introduction and chapter 39

Keller, H. (n.d.) "Helen Keller Quotes" (n.d)

https://sites.psu.edu/kristenraschello/

Chapter 7

Auto Safety

https://www.autosafety.org/ford-pinto-fuel-tank/

Chapter 8

Defense Casualty Analysis System (2022) "U.S.Military Casualties-Vietnam Conflict Casualty Summary

https://www.archives.gov/research/military/vietnam-war/casualty-statistics#toc--dcas-vietnam-conflict-extract-file-record-counts-by-casualty-country-over-water-code-country-of-casualty-as-of-april-29-2008--2**https://www.nps.gov/gari/planyourvisit/whitewater.htm**

Chapter 28

Gauley River

https://www.nps.gov/gari/index.htm

REFERENCES

Chapter 31

Mind

https://en.m.wikipedia.org/wiki/Mind#:~:text=The%20mind%20is%20often%20understood,with%20body%2C%20matter%20or%20physicality

Chapter 39

Notre Dame

https://www.usnews.com/best-colleges/university-of-notre-dame-1840/overall-rankings